Charles Colson

rwin McManus

Max Lucado

Bob Russell

Zig Ziglar

z Curtis Higgs

byjon Caldwell

Rob Bell

anklin Graham

...and more!

refining your STYLE

Learning From Respected Communicators

storyteller   persuasive motivator   scholarly analytic   revolutionary leader   passionate teacher   convincing apologist   relevant urban

DaVE STONE

Group
Loveland, Colorado

I0651110

Refining Your Style: Learning From Respected Communicators
Copyright © 2004 Dave Stone

Visit our Web site: **www.grouppublishing.com**

Credits
Senior Acquisitions Editor: Brian Proffit
Editor: Debbie Gowensmith
Chief Creative Officer: Joani Schultz
Copy Editor: Ann M. Diaz
Art Director: Pamela Poll
Designer: Pamela Poll
Cover Art Director: Jeff A. Storm
Cover Designer: Alan Furst Inc.
Production Manager: Peggy Naylor

Library of Congress Cataloging-in-Publication Data
Stone, Dave, 1961-
  Refining your style : learning from respected communicators / by Dave Stone.-- 1st American pbk. ed.
     p. cm.
  Includes bibliographical references.
  ISBN 0-7644-2682-6 (pbk. : alk. paper)
  1. Communication--Religious aspects--Christianity. 2. Preaching.
I. Title.
  BV4319.S675 2004
  251--dc22
                                        2004003875

ISBN 0-7644-2682-6

10 9 8 7 6 5 4 3 2 1   13 12 11 10 09 08 07 06 05 04

Printed in the United States of America.

Dedication

This book is dedicated to **Bob Russell,** my mentor, friend, and hero in the faith.

Your passion for preaching, your life of integrity, your commitment to the truth of God's Word, and your personal encouragement motivate me more than you'll ever know.

Your influence is sprinkled throughout each page of this book. Thanks for taking a chance on a twenty-seven-year-old rookie and investing fifteen-plus years into his life. Above all, thanks for being the same man at home, work, and play that you are in the pulpit.

Acknowledgments

Beth, Savannah, Sadie, and Samuel: Thanks for being patient with me through some late evenings on this project. I love you each very much.

Group Publishing—Debbie Gowensmith, Candace McMahan, Dave Thornton, and Brian Proffit: You all at Group Publishing are awesome. Thanks for stretching me in my writing and for believing in me!

Thanks for the encouragement and help from the following super servants: Debbie Carper, Dana Pinkston, Marty Anderson, Sam and Gwen Stone, Jeff and Johnnie Stone, Bobby Bowman, Matt Proctor, Mark Jones, Phil Gambill, Mike Shannon, Rick Rusaw, Paul Williams, Bob Shank, Joe Bonura, Cameron McDonald, Kyle Idleman, Rusty Russell, Dave Kennedy, Gregg Dedrick, David Enyart, Chad Doerr, Evan Meyer, Irv White, and Steve Metts.

Contents

Introduction

I LOVE TO COMMUNICATE THE MESSAGE OF GOD'S LOVE TO PEOPLE. I love to share with others the difference Christ has made in my life. The Apostle Paul aptly described the passion of my heart when he wrote, "Woe to me if I do not preach the gospel" (1 Corinthians 9:16). Since I felt the Lord confirm my calling to teach and preach the Word, not a day has gone by that I haven't thought of how I could be more effective in reaching people with the knowledge of Christ.

You have, too, or you wouldn't have picked up this book and CD. Whether you lead a home Bible study, teach a Sunday school class, or preach to masses, you desire to communicate the good news as effectively as you can.

As always, such an awesome privilege is tempered by incredible responsibility. Communicating the gospel is a "joyful burden."[1] Regardless of class size or the number of people in the sanctuary, those who teach or lead must take adequate time to prepare their content and practice their delivery. James' warning, "Not many of you should presume to be teachers" (James 3:1), adds to the pressure you already feel in serving fresh bread to a spiritually starved world. The ongoing task of trying to make old truths come alive can be frustrating.

The purpose is not to become like these communicators but to see which communication styles you identify with.

With God's blessing and by familiarizing yourself with your natural communication style, you can communicate more effectively—starting today. Whether you are already serving as a lay leader or paid minister or are pursuing vocational ministry at a college or seminary, *Refining Your Style* will provide opportunities to learn from some of the best-known Christian communicators in the country.

The purpose is not to become like these communicators but to see which communication styles you identify with. *I encourage you to be yourself.*

In a workshop on preaching, Fred Craddock quickly set me at ease by saying, "This is the way I've chosen to do things. This is my style. I won't paint my number on your jersey and put you into the game. You have your own jersey."[2]

Accordingly, this book is not designed to drastically change your personal style. If you've golfed for twenty years and then take lessons, a wise instructor won't radically alter your swing. He may make minor adjustments, but he always will work with what comes naturally for you. If you're a fan of a particular golfer, you might *try* to imitate that player's swing. Down deep you realize that Tiger Woods may influence the way you try to swing, but no one will ever mistake you for Tiger. Ever. You have a style all your own.

The same is true for communicating. You may not become the next Erwin McManus or Liz Curtis Higgs. That's OK. As Carl Hurley once said, "We spend most of our lives trying to be someone else, and yet God made us all originals. You are the only one who can be *you* and get it right!"[3]

Oh, how Christian authors, preachers, and teachers could benefit from resting in such a simple truth. Psalm 139 underscores your uniqueness: "God knit you together in your mother's womb. Praise God because you are fearfully and wonderfully made!"

Just being yourself is easier said than done, though, because Satan whispers to you, "You don't measure up."

Just being yourself is easier said than done, though, because Satan whispers to you, "You don't measure up."

Brennan Manning said, "When I was eight...the impostor, or false self, was born as a defense against pain. The impostor within whispered, 'Brennan, don't ever be your real self anymore because nobody likes you as you are. Invent a new self that everybody will admire and nobody will know.'"[4]

That mindset sticks with us, sometimes long into adulthood. Within a matter of months of beginning my preaching career at Southeast Christian Church, I had fallen into a habit I had vowed to avoid. I had unknowingly begun to copy my mentor and senior minister, Bob Russell. The cadence, inflection, and style were *his*. Bob sat me down and lovingly said, "We didn't hire you to be another Bob Russell. We already have one of those. We hired you because you are Dave Stone. You have talents and a style that allow you to reach some people I can't reach. Just be yourself."

Bob never had to tell me that again. I cannot tell you how liberating it was to learn that God could use me just the way he had formed and made me. At the same time, I realized that the Holy Spirit could sharpen my strengths and help me to overcome some of my limitations.

If you're new to teaching and preaching, your communication style may yet be incubating.

I've written this book so that you can experience the same freedom I did. You can communicate in the way God has gifted you. Your church doesn't ask you to be Max Lucado, Franklin Graham, or Bill Hybels. *They ask you to teach or preach because you are you.* They, like God, see incredible potential in you. They firmly believe God can use you to communicate truth.

When you follow your natural inclination, empowered by the Holy Spirit, Satan had better watch out. God used a stuttering murderer named Moses to communicate to masses of Israelites and a powerful king. Recall an introverted, soft-spoken fisherman named Andrew who brought many people—including his brother Simon Peter—to Christ. Remember how God transformed an antagonist named Saul into an evangelist named Paul. Look at the impact Jabez, an obscure Old Testament character, has had—with a little help from Bruce Wilkinson!

If you're new to teaching or preaching, your communication style may yet be incubating. Personal mentors and well-known speakers are influencing you. Those of you who have been "in the business" for decades may be set in your style. Perhaps *too* set. For all of us, the biggest room in the house is the room for improvement. By presenting examples of excellent Christian communicators, this book seeks to help you develop the gifts God has given you and overcome some of your weaknesses.

Each of us communicates with a mixture of styles. You'll find yourself in a number of the following chapters, and you'll be intrigued by styles unfamiliar to you. Most of us will have to employ every single style in this book at some point, so stretch yourself if a particular style isn't natural for you. To help you discover and refine your very own style—and to help you grow in those styles that are unfamiliar to you—each chapter includes the following:

1. An introduction to the style

I'll acquaint you with what this style looks and sounds like. Through quotes, Scriptures, and comparisons, you'll begin to understand the chapter's specific communication style.

2. An explanation of how Jesus utilized the style

Jesus Christ was the *master* communicator. Throughout his ministry, he employed every one of the communication styles found in this book. He seemed to know just which one to utilize and when to do so. In each chapter, you'll be reminded of how Jesus matched his style with the particular needs of the people.

3. Interviews with Christian communicators

Some of today's best Christian communicators candidly share their calling to ministry, their styles, their struggles, and their speaking and teaching disciplines. They come from different denominations, backgrounds, and ministries. As you read their honest self-evaluations and communication goals, your respect and appreciation for each communicator will increase even more.

You'll learn for whom Lee Strobel writes every sermon that he preaches. You'll be amazed at who used to hyperventilate in seventh grade when he had to read out loud. You'll even meet a guy whose punk rock band was the grassroots network for starting a church. (No, it's not Chuck Colson!) You'll be shocked to learn which of our featured communicators was personally chided by none other than Howard Stern for outrageous and immoral behavior years ago. You'll also hear about Zig Ziglar's preparation routine before delivering a talk.

I would be remiss if I failed to mention how humble and gracious every one of these featured communicators has been to me. Each of these servants was generous with time and expressed appreciation for being included in the project. Each invested more than an hour of valuable time to help you and me become more effective communicators of this "treasure" (2 Corinthians 4:7). Most said they felt out of place with such quality communicators. After each interview I thought, *"Is it any wonder God has blessed the ministries of these folks?"*

4. Advice on refining each style
Every style has strengths to be accentuated and weaknesses to avoid. Each chapter offers pithy, practical tips and cautions that can refine your communication skills.

5. Biblical exposition
Rather than setting apart a particular style as Biblical Expositor, I felt that the art of breaking down Scripture and explaining it is paramount to every communication style in this book. Therefore you will find thoughts and tips on expository teaching and preaching woven throughout the book as they relate to each particular style.

Refining Your Style also includes "Styles at a Glance." These shaded pages, located just after this introduction, provide you with a summation of the featured communicators and their styles. Refer to this on a regular basis to help you differentiate the styles. Take a look at "Featured Communicators' Self-Descriptions" (p. 14) to see which styles the featured communicators selected as their own. After reading the book, you can evaluate your own natural style. Determine which communicators are most like *you*. (Thanks to Matt Proctor, preaching professor at Ozark Christian College, Joplin, Missouri, for his input on the wording.)

The accompanying *Refining Your Style* CD completes the package. You'll hear actual clips from as many of the featured communicators as we could fit on one compact disc! Hearing these respected communicators in action is a wonderful opportunity that also increases your takeaway. I suggest that you listen to the CD while you're reading the book and then again after you've completed it. Remember, it never hurts to pick up some new illustrations and ideas!

So read on and listen on. Find some similarities between yourself and some expert Christian communicators. Allow the Lord to mold you and make you after his will—*not theirs*.

The Apostle Paul assures us that "he who began a good work in you will carry it on to completion until the day of Christ Jesus" (Philippians 1:6).

In other words, this is a "come as you are" party. In the following pages, a variety of people will remind you to *be yourself*—the best self you can be with the help of the Lord and the Holy Spirit.

One more thing: *Keep your own jersey.* It will work just fine.

ENDNOTES

1 Fred Craddock, "Preaching Workshop #1" (Indianapolis, IN: North American Christian Convention, July 10, 2003).

2 Craddock, "Preaching Workshop #1."

3 Carl Hurley, comments (Indianapolis, IN: Praise Gathering, 1990).

4 John Eldredge, *Wild at Heart: Discovering the Secret of a Man's Soul* (Nashville, TN: Thomas Nelson, Inc., 2001), 107.

Styles at a Glance
The Thirteen Styles of Communication

A summary developed by Dave Stone and Matt Proctor.

STYLE	PURPOSE	TARGET	FEATURED COMMUNICATOR
Creative Storyteller	Speaks to help people *visualize* something.	The listener's *imagination*	Max Lucado
Direct Spokesperson	Speaks to help people *decide* something.	The listener's *will*	Franklin Graham
Scholarly Analytic	Speaks to help people *understand* something.	The listener's *logic*	Tim Keller
Revolutionary Leader	Speaks to help people *ignite* something.	The listener's *passion*	Erwin McManus
Engaging Humorist	Speaks to help people *enjoy* something.	The listener's *funny bone*	Ken Davis
Convincing Apologist	Speaks to help people *believe* something.	The listener's *worldview*	Lee Strobel
Inspiring Orator	Speaks to help people *feel* something.	The listener's *emotions*	Kirbyjon Caldwell

STYLE	PURPOSE	TARGET	FEATURED COMMUNICATOR
Practical Applicator	Speaks to help people implement something.	The listener's habits	Bob Russell
Persuasive Motivator	Speaks to help people transform something.	The listener's attitude	Zig Ziglar
Passionate Teacher	Speaks to help people learn something.	The listener's mind	Liz Curtis Higgs
Relevant Illustrator	Speaks to help people connect with something.	The listener's common sense	Gene Appel
Cultural Prophet	Speaks to help people confront something.	The listener's conscience	Chuck Colson
Unorthodox Artist	Speaks to help people experience something.	The listener's senses	Rob Bell

Featured Communicators' Self-Descriptions

I showed each communicator the list of the thirteen styles presented in this book. Below you'll find the styles that each communicator chose to reflect his or her own natural style. Do you see yourself in some of them?

COMMUNICATOR	SELF-SELECTED STYLES
Gene Appel	Relevant Illustrator, Inspiring Orator, Persuasive Motivator, Practical Applicator, Passionate Teacher
Rob Bell	Unorthodox Artist, Passionate Teacher, Creative Storyteller (Being unorthodox, Rob also coined these terms to describe himself: Mind Stretcher, Question Asker, Fundamentalist Frustrator.)
Kirbyjon Caldwell	Inspiring Orator, Persuasive Motivator, Direct Spokesperson, Revolutionary Leader, Passionate Teacher
Chuck Colson	Cultural Prophet, Convincing Apologist, Scholarly Analytic, Persuasive Motivator
Ken Davis	Engaging Humorist, Persuasive Motivator, Creative Storyteller, Relevant Illustrator
Franklin Graham	Direct Spokesperson, Persuasive Motivator, Relevant Illustrator, Creative Storyteller
Liz Curtis Higgs	Passionate Teacher, Creative Storyteller, Engaging Humorist, Unorthodox Artist

COMMUNICATOR	SELF-SELECTED STYLES
Tim Keller	Scholarly Analytic, Convincing Apologist, Practical Applicator
Max Lucado	Creative Storyteller, Persuasive Motivator, Relevant Illustrator, Inspiring Orator
Erwin McManus	Revolutionary Leader, Unorthodox Artist, Cultural Prophet (Erwin also described himself as a Mystic Warrior.)
Bob Russell	Practical Applicator, Relevant Illustrator, Direct Spokesperson, Scholarly Analytic
Dave Stone	Persuasive Motivator, Relevant Illustrator, Engaging Humorist, Inspiring Orator
Lee Strobel	Convincing Apologist, Passionate Teacher, Persuasive Motivator, Relevant Illustrator, Creative Storyteller
Zig Ziglar	Persuasive Motivator, Practical Applicator, Passionate Teacher, Creative Storyteller, Cultural Prophet

CHAPTER 1

The Creative Storyteller

"One might *think* a deductive sermon into existence, but story sermons must be *thought and felt* into existence. Deductive sermons march with the precision of soldiers at boot camp; narrative sermons *dance* their way into the world."
—David A. Enyart[1]

"With many similar parables Jesus spoke the word to them, as much as they could understand. He did not say anything to them without using a parable. But when he was alone with his own disciples, he explained everything." —Mark 4:33-34

The Creative Storyteller speaks to help people *visualize* something.
The target is the listener's *imagination*.
Think Max Lucado.

Similar styles: Engaging Humorist, Unorthodox Artist, Persuasive Motivator, Inspiring Orator

Words that describe this style: Clever, charming, childlike, clear, right-brained, talented, entertaining

You might be a Creative Storyteller if...
- you see a movie and, by your captivating description of scenes, can make others feel as if they were there.
- outlining is secondary to the flow of the message.
- you're more concerned about resonating with the heart than the head.
- your listeners feel as if they know you and your family inside and out because of the compelling stories you've shared.

About This Style

Russ Blowers, a long-time minister in Indianapolis, was also active in the Rotary. Each week a different club member would briefly introduce himself, including his job and responsibilities. But Russ thought it sounded so bland and boring to say, "I'm a minister." When it was his week to introduce himself, Russ stood up and said the following:

> Hi, I'm Russ Blowers. I'm with a global enterprise. We have branches in every country in the world. We're into motivation and behavior alteration. We run hospitals, feeding stations, crisis pregnancy centers, universities, publishing houses, and nursing homes. We care for our clients from birth to death.
>
> We are into life insurance and fire insurance. We perform spiritual heart transplants. Our original Organizer owns all the real estate on earth plus an assortment of galaxies and constellations. He knows everything and lives everywhere. Our product is free for the asking.
>
> Our CEO was born in a hick town, worked as a carpenter, didn't own a home, was misunderstood by his family, was hated by his enemies, walked on water, was condemned to death, and arose from the dead. I talk with him every day.[2]

You would assume that Russ' explanation was one of the most memorable. Rather than spouting off a linear list—name of church, location, years served, and so on—Russ told a story that captured interest and opened the door for questions and counsel in the months to come.

As you lead a Bible study group or preach from a pulpit, never underestimate the magnetic appeal of a well-told story.

As you lead a Bible study group or preach from a pulpit, never underestimate the magnetic appeal of a well-told story. You can effectively cast a spell on your listeners. A mesmerizing account can have an overwhelming spiritual impact on people, and many people need stories to help them understand some truth. Clark Tanner says, "Points are for the head; stories are for the heart."[3]

Storytelling makes your message more memorable. Sometimes when I speak for a main convention session and am following with a workshop on preaching, I'll do this exercise: In the workshop, I'll ask the audience to repeat the key points of my previous session's outline. Usually a few can, but honestly most can't. Then I'll ask who could retell, for example, the bungee-jumping joke I opened with. Every hand goes up. I ask, "How many of you think you could repeat the story I told about the elderly lady in Cincinnati?" Again the hands go up. "How about the story about my son Samuel's first day at school?" I ask. Once again, all hands go up. This is the value of stories.

No wonder creative storytelling is becoming one of the more popular styles. In *Creative Anticipation*, one of the best books available on storytelling and narratives, David A. Enyart offers this one-paragraph explanation of this style's effectiveness:

> With [narrative preaching], the listener reasons alongside the preacher, moving simultaneously toward conclusions. The narrative sermon *arrives at* a universal thesis toward the end of the message, rather than asserting it at the beginning...Induction creatively *pulls* the hearer onward with an unresolved conflict or unanswered question. With inductive sermon designs, speaker and listener walk side by side in search of God's answer to a specific problem or conflict.[4]

In *Laughter, Tears, and In-Between*, Paul S. Williams shares an example of the power of stories from his own life:

> I remember Dad lying next to our beds telling stories about cowboys Jim and Jiggles to my brother and me. I never knew he was making up the stories line by line as he told them. I just lay there breathlessly, glancing every now and then at my Hopalong Cassidy watch, knowing that although it looked bleak, somehow in the next ten minutes the good guys were gonna win. A gasp from my brother would send Dad down one story line. A yawn from me and he'd yank out a subplot. To me the stories seemed well told, with characters perfectly developed in love...
>
> I speak often on camera, as well as to small audiences and large audiences around the country. I get nervous before I speak, but I settle in when I tell the first story. The stories don't illustrate my points. They are my points.[5]

Again, the message of this book is just to be yourself! Some may have great gifts of creativity but don't do well with narratives.

Others can tell a story well but lack the inventiveness and imagination to inject, week in and week out, the peaks and valleys a good story needs. Still others prefer to link several short stories together with Scriptures and applications. No matter how you use them, stories are powerful because they work their way beneath the surface.

No matter how you use them, stories are powerful because they work their way beneath the surface.

Someone once asked Calvin Miller why he moved away from didactic, precept-driven, three-point sermons toward story sermons. He explained, "I finally came to say, 'Miller, that's just not who you are.' There are some who can do it well, and for whom that is a natural style, but it was not me. The style has to be native to the preacher."[6] Miller realized his style didn't need to fit in neatly with the majority's deductive assembly line and that he would be more effective following his natural bent. So will you!

Storytelling may not feel natural for you, but you have to admit that it adds incredible value—especially to efforts in reaching the postmodern generations. While you may not become a narrative preacher, you can still sprinkle some stories into your teaching. It will require tedious preparation, ongoing practice, and honest critique and encouragement from others. Practice telling stories Monday through Friday. It may become addictive—for you and for your listeners. You'll often hear your congregation or students say, "Your story really touched me."

When I present seminars on communication, invariably someone will ask, "Where do you get your illustrations and stories?" While the question is a good one, perhaps a better one is "How do you tell a story so people will listen and learn?" Let's learn the answer from those who know best.

Jesus, a Creative Storyteller

Paul S. Williams writes, "I'm told we humans can't sleep without dreaming. And when was the last time you had a dream that wasn't in story form?…The need for story is downright physiological."[7] Jesus knew that. After all, Jesus was there when God created humans in his image. While the Master Communicator spoke in Luke 15, he watched the light come on as his listeners' minds drifted to something they had lost—a coin, a sheep, a wayward child.

Jesus utilized every one of the communication styles in this book, but I think he enjoyed this one the most. He mesmerized thousands of people by telling practical stories mixed with spiritual applications. He told farm stories. He told relationship stories. He told money stories. These parables caused people to think, "Wow, this guy is talking my language." We can search high and low for the tricks of the storytelling trade, but the best examples are in the Gospels.

Max Lucado, a Creative Storyteller

Storytelling can't be covered without mentioning names like Calvin Miller, Haddon Robinson, and Fred Craddock.[8] But in the last fifteen years, a new name has emerged. You can probably see that name on a book sitting on a nearby shelf—a book that contains captivating story after captivating story. Max Lucado takes his stories from the same events that happen to you and me, but his creativity brings them to life.

Max is unusually talented. A switch-hitter, he can say it *or* write it as effectively as anyone can. Selling more than thirty million copies of your books is a fairly good indicator that your style resonates with people! Part of Max's appeal is his simple, creative approach to narrative preaching.

While people across the nation know Max as an author, several thousand people in San Antonio, Texas, refer to him as "pastor." Max knows the pressure of preparing and delivering quality new material because he does it week in and week out, preaching nearly forty-five weekends a year at Oak Hills Church. In addition, Max is expected to turn out a new book or two each year.

Max's natural style has remained unchanged over the past twenty-five years, but he has continued to improve and sharpen his speaking skills. Just as in his books, his mainstay is storytelling. He's a preacher, an author, and—most important, from my vantage point—a faithful friend.

Interview With Max Lucado

DAVE: When did you first realize you had the gift of communication?

MAX: Back in west Texas at Andrews High School, I found that public speaking came easily. I discovered that I enjoyed writing. I signed up for speech teams, joined the debate team, signed up for "ready writing" competitions that were similar to extemporaneous speaking. I thought it was really fun, so I realized early on that I could stand in front of people.

The very first time I ran for office, I built my campaign speech around a story—a real common story about a father who had twelve sons. He gave each son a stick and told him to go and set it on fire. They did, and they came back and said, "Wasn't much." Then the father said, "Now take all twelve sticks and put them together." And the sons learned what happens when we all work together. It's just a sweet story. I can remember telling that story, watching people, and thinking, "They're really listening to me." I began realizing that there's power in a well-told story that sticks with people.

DAVE: How did this tie in with your spiritual journey?

MAX: My spiritual journey really began in college, so I'm not sure when I began to understand that what I was doing for academics could be used spiritually. I think I was about twenty-one the first time I was asked to speak out of the Bible. I had gone back to our home church, and they asked me to give a devotional. That was the first time I'd spoken at any event for any cause other than my own. There was a real sense of satisfaction.

DAVE: What communicators have influenced your style?

MAX: That's a great question. I remember the storytellers. I can still remember the stories of a young fellow in west Texas whose name is Jerry Browning. He's gone on to heaven now, but he told stories that would just grab me. A great man named Lynn Anderson, who's actually in our church now, is another. Lee Strobel interviewed him for a book. When I was in college going through my spiritual discoveries, Lynn preached all the way through the Gospel of John. I can remember his stories. Powerful stories.

DAVE: Have you always gravitated toward storytelling?

MAX: Well, I remember that my earliest sermon outlines were stories—five stories linked together. I linked them so I could remember my points! I'd first tell a story, then make an application, then tell another story that made my point.

Through the years, I've just found that stories endear you to people. They take you from a classroom to a living room. They evoke emotion, whether laughter or tears. They get to the head *through* the heart.

Last Sunday, for example, I told a story about a fly I saw in an airplane. It struck me: What was a fly doing flying in an airplane? So I made this stupid, crazy sentence: "Why does a fly in a plane fly in a plane?" I was really proud of that sentence, and I had the whole church laughing *at* me just as much as they were laughing *with* me. Then I interviewed the fly. I said, "Why don't you settle down?"

He said, "'Cause I'm holding this whole thing up."

And I said, "You're not either." By that point in the story, people were laughing.

I've found that the line following the story is the most important line. I really spend a lot of time thinking about how I'm going to transition to my point because people are laughing and goofy. So last Sunday, I said, "The fly told me to buzz off. He didn't listen to me."

Then I said, "But I oh-so hope you will."[9] Just that little transition right there. Then I said, "We don't have to spend our lives frantically waving our wings. God's holding us up. We can sit down and rest in him and trust him to carry us."

> "I've found that the line following the story is the most important line."

My experience has been that a story gives people a memory—a hook—to hang onto. Stories can do as much or more than some analytical thinking for most of the people in the pew. Some people are kind of analytical by nature, but I think most people love stories. Even this week, two or three people have said to me, "That fly story was so crazy." But they remembered it.

DAVE: What is the biggest challenge for you to overcome due to your natural style? What do you have to guard against to discipline yourself?

MAX: I have to guard against puffy, purely entertaining sermons with no depth to them, no scriptural exposition. I've guarded against that by listening to good expository preachers. I remember listening to a couple of John Stott's sermons—one in person—and realizing he did not use one sermon illustration. Not one story. When I saw him in person, he never stepped away from the pulpit but had twelve hundred of us eating out of the palm of his hand because he was so carefully exposing the Word of God. So I have listened to John MacArthur tapes and John Stott tapes and have read books by careful students. I don't know if I've succeeded or not, but that's the challenge to me.

> "I have to guard against puffy, purely entertaining sermons with no depth to them, no scriptural exposition."

DAVE: I know you manuscript your messages, but do you practice them out loud?

MAX: I do manuscript, but I don't practice messages out loud. I read over them. I sit with them. During the first service, I'm standing there with the message in front of me. By the second, I'm rolling a little bit. But by the third service, I'm not flipping pages anymore.

DAVE: What descriptive words would your church members use to describe your preaching?

MAX: Gentle. I don't yell at the church. I assume they want to learn or they wouldn't be there. I'm not sure all ministers assume that. I also assume, as Charles Spurgeon said, "There's a broken heart in every pew." Just preach like there's somebody there who is right at the end of their rope. If I preach to that person, I'll catch a lot of people on this side of desperation.

DAVE: Now, how would *you* describe your preaching?

MAX: Pastoral. Shepherding. Nurturing. Mildly evangelistic. I want to be more evangelistic, but I keep finding myself going back to being more nurturing and pastoral and comforting.

DAVE: You've been preaching for twenty-five years now. How has your preaching style changed?

MAX: Initially, I think I was a loud preacher because I had grown up hearing a lot of loud preaching. By necessity I had to soften up because I got vocal nodules. That's when I started wearing the wraparound, Garth Brooks microphone!

I think I've gotten a little softer, more gentle. I want to think that I've become more well-rounded in terms of good scriptural messages complemented by stories; I used to use lots of good stories complemented by a verse or two. I think I'm stronger at expository. And as much as I enjoy preaching, I'm still very insecure and don't feel like I do a very good job. On Mondays I always think, "Boy, that was stupid."

DAVE: Writing sermons is an ongoing pressure. My preacher friend Rick Rusaw recently said to me, "Preaching is like giving birth Sunday and waking up Monday morning and finding out you're pregnant again!"

MAX: My predecessor, who's now at Abilene Christian University, is a really neat guy named Jack Reese. He told me once about his biggest surprise his first Sunday at his first church. He had worked and worked and worked to get the sermon ready. He preached it, and then that night he realized he had to do it all over again the next week! (Laughter.)

DAVE: It just didn't occur to him! Now let's change gears. Your writing has allowed you to have a larger platform in speaking nationally. I watched you recently on tour with Michael W. Smith and Third Day. You have always been a great preacher, but you seemed to have stepped it up a notch. Your transitions were masterful. Even with ten thousand to fifteen thousand people all around, it somehow still seemed that you were talking right to me.

MAX: But you know in those situations, Dave, I feel like—this is a Bill Hybels phrase—somebody gave me the football on the other team's two-yard line! The music was so strong, the people's hearts were there, they were all worshipping. The worship was honest, I perceived. Everything said, "Worship, worship, worship." So by the time I stood up there, people's hearts were soft and pliable. They weren't resistant. They were thrilled to be there.

And all they wanted somebody to do was put an exclamation point on it. Or maybe give a little bit of teaching. So I felt like it was an easy job. I didn't have to woo the audience and win them over.

DAVE: Do you see yourself more as a preacher who writes or as a writer who preaches?

MAX: The stock answer to that question is "I hope I never have to choose." I really think if I make any long-lasting contributions to the kingdom, it will be through writing. It will be the books that are here long after I'm gone. Also, I don't see myself as a really strong church builder as I look at others—like Bob Russell—as a church builder.[10]

DAVE: I want to be true to what your thoughts are. Several years ago, I was driving you and your elders back to the Louisville airport. You may recall that I asked them, "Is Max a writer who preaches or a preacher who writes?" Immediately and in unison they all said, "Max is a preacher who writes."

MAX: I guess it all depends on how we define *preacher*. When I think "preacher," I think "church leader." "Senior minister." "Visionary." But I do love to preach!

DAVE: This morning in a workshop on preaching, Fred Craddock said, "I love the preparation. I hate the delivery."[11] In the sermonic process, what comes most naturally for you—preparation or delivery?

MAX: I guess I'm blessed because I love the whole process. I love the preparation. I love the presentation.

I catch myself always preparing sermons in my head, outlining sermons in my head, looking at verses in my head. Like a lot of presenters, I have to be careful that my personal devotionals don't become preparation time. My favorite day of the week is the day I clear just to study and prepare. I know it's going to be tough. I know I'll get stumped a lot. But I'll get in there and slug it out and know that the Lord will bring me through and there will be something there at the end of the day.

Then I feel excitement when it's time to stand and speak.

DAVE: Part of speaking is writing quality material. I can't close

> "Like a lot of presenters, I have to be careful that my personal devotionals don't become preparation time."

this interview until I ask you to share some tips on writing for those church leaders who aspire to be authors.

MAX: I think the most overlooked principle of writing is *rewriting*. The best writers are rewriters. They rewrite over and over and over. An article I read in 1985, just when my first book had come out, really got me thinking about this. A Reader's Digest article about Ernest Hemingway said he rewrote *The Old Man and the Sea* dozens of times. Each day he would begin by rewriting what he'd written the day before, which would take him nearly the whole day! He'd usually have about thirty minutes left to write new material. Hemingway would start over and rewrite it again and rewrite it again and rewrite it again.

That kind of rewriting really hones down the project. You see it with fresh eyes. You see needless verbs.

My daughters are being taught to go back and take out as many "be" verbs as possible. Instead of saying a predictable sentence like "He is a good man," you try to come up with something a lot stronger—"John echoed kindness."

Sometimes I pick up a book, and it just seems like a B+ book. The message might be great, but you think, "Boy, I wish he had gone one more round with it." Rewriting is tough because it takes time. You've got to get to the point that you're so sick of the manuscript!

DAVE: Everything you've said applies to writing a manuscript for preaching as well.

MAX: That's so true. I think the best counsel I've received on preaching is to try to distill the whole sermon into one sentence. I read a story in a preaching book about a man whose son became a minister. The father's assignment for his son was this: Every Saturday night, his son was to send Dad the essence of his sermon in a ten-word telegraph. That was the father's way of making sure the son had focused his thoughts so much that he could put his sermon into a sentence.

That, to me, is the challenge. When I try to make too many points, I don't make any one of them well. My better sermons are the ones in which I repeat a phrase again and again—"Nothing can separate us from the love of Christ." You come at that point from every angle, from top to bottom. Then you find stories that strengthen the point rather than liking a story so much that you're trying to find a point to fit it. I've done that, too!

For those of you who feel you have a lot of improving to do, maybe this will inspire you. Max Lucado sent his first book manuscript to publisher after publisher. The *fifteenth* said "yes." That book was *On the Anvil*. This lesson in perseverance also shows Max's willingness to open himself up to criticism and rejection.

Advice on Refining This Style
◆ *Search and sift for quality stories.*
As is true when hunting for sand crabs on the beach at night, diligence and patience in finding stories will pay off. Read newspapers, periodicals, church papers. Listen to newscasts and to storytellers such as Paul Harvey on the radio. Surf the Web for illustrations. If a story touches you, you know it can touch someone else. Take notes on every talk, lesson, or sermon you hear. Jot down each story's main details. Then make certain you keep your notes, organized by topic, where you can retrieve them. This way, you can find and use the story when you need it.

> If a story touches you, you know it can touch someone else.

◆ *Craft your stories to hold attention.*
To effectively tell stories, you must be able to get the listeners' attention, hold it through tension or conflict, and then tie together all the pieces. Not an easy task. One tip is to imagine you're telling the story to a child at bedtime. In that setting, you use expressions and voices—whatever it takes—to give the child something to ponder long after the story is over. The element of surprise or an unexpected twist goes a long way toward keeping listeners tuned in.

◆ *Weave a particular point throughout the entire message.*
Too many deductive lessons or sermons try to drive home too many points. The main theme gets lost. The listener is more apt

to move toward some specific life change if the approach is more focused. While drinking from a fire hydrant may be fun, it's more disorienting than quenching your thirst at a drinking fountain!

Like a musical chord or interlude introduced early in a musical and then repeated throughout, a repeated point or phrase helps listeners with recall. For example, you may mention the point in the introduction, throughout the message, and again during the conclusion; I derive incredible fulfillment from playing the conclusion back to the introduction. People tend to remember stories, so it's easier for them to recall points expressed through stories than through some other section of your sermon or lesson.

◆ Don't rely on your "gift of gab."

Over the long haul, verbal competencies can't hide a lack of preparation. Storytelling should be an outgrowth of your study and prep time. Winging it reduces the potency of your lessons. It also gives the speaker the misleading perception that he or she can "pull this off" without much preparation. Therein lies the difference between a good storyteller and a great one.

◆ Refine your stories.

Stories must be seen as a work in progress. Think about what you hope to communicate throughout the entire week. Then rewrite. Refine. Excellent storytelling requires careful crafting, relentless editing, and wordsmithing. Shortcuts in these areas will make your message memorable for the wrong reasons! As you write, think of the order in which you want the audience to hear the details of the story. Concentrate on descriptive words. Eliminate extraneous words along with repetition, redundancy, and repeating yourself. (That last phrase was a test to make certain you're paying attention!) With such diligence, the essence of the story will improve along with the takeaway of the entire message.

> **Excellent storytelling requires careful crafting, relentless editing, and wordsmithing.**

◆ Pepper your stories with imagery.

Use words in your stories that help listeners visualize the action.

Describe the sights, the sounds, the smells. For example, instead of saying "an indentation," say "a softball-sized dent."

Peter Marshall, a chaplain for the U.S. Senate, was a firm believer in this. It's reported that "in his lectures on preaching, Marshall emphasized the importance of using verbal stimulation for visual imagery. He advocated word painting in which the preacher used his verbal skills to 'Turn the ear into an eye.'"[12]

♦ *Watch the transitions.*

Put as much time crafting the transitions into and out of the story as you do the actual story. When you listen to the CD accompanying this book, you'll hear Max's artful transitions from the stories to his message's primary point. You want the entire finished product to flow together. Think seamless! Like a chain, your message is only as strong as the links that hold it together.

Your eyes and facial expressions communicate your fervor for the story you're sharing.

♦ *Better eye contact = better storytelling.*

In critique sessions after Saturday night sermons, my respected compadres have said to me, "When you're telling a story, look up and engage us with your eyes. You know the story well enough, so there's no reason to look down at your notes. Enjoy telling it."

Eye contact helps you to connect with your audience and hold their attention. (See Chuck Colson's comments on eye contact in the Cultural Prophet chapter.) Even the best narrative will die an early death if you are unfamiliar with your notes. Your eyes and facial expressions communicate your fervor for the story you're sharing.

♦ *Convey your passion for the story.*

If you are passionate about a story, the audience will listen passionately. Conversely, if you're not into a story, don't expect your audience to be. Listeners can sense quite quickly whether you're passionate about the stories you share.

When asked how to encourage preachers to develop a narrative style of communication, Calvin Miller said this:

I do agree that some people are natural storytellers, but…I've heard professional athletes, especially right after they become Christians, tell their story. They look down, they're weak, they use no significant adjectives, they don't know how to construct a story in any kind of literary form—they just tell what happened to them in Jesus. It's sweet and it's wonderful. They begin to cry, their lip quivers, their chin drops, and they lose control. Everything about what they do says, "This is not literary; it's not good," but there's an emotive power of the existential moment—*what happened to me* is what really communicates.

If you want to develop a narrative kind of style, try to remember that, whether right-brained or left-brained, all people have to tell somebody what's happened to them. The guy who's maybe such a jock that he's never read a novel or short story can still tell his wife what happened to him during the day. And when he's telling her, she listens. Maybe he's not a great storyteller, but he's into his story.[13]

◆ *Use stories to stimulate discussion.*

Rob Bell, the featured Unorthodox Artist, concluded his interview with me by saying, "I think great preaching *begins* the discussion, not *ends* it." Your message should be a launching pad for spiritual conversations in the days to come, and memorable stories do this effectively.

Richard Jensen, two days after preaching a narrative sermon, received a visit from a seminary student who had heard the sermon. The student told Jensen that narrative preaching was flawed because he had debated the meaning of the sermon with another student for two hours without reaching consensus. Jensen responded with happiness that his sermon had led to such a deep discussion.[14]

Stories can catch listeners off-guard with an unexpected ending, weave together discordant threads, and even end without wrapping the message in a tidy package. Such stories can lead listeners into great discussions, which often is a more favorable outcome than letting them walk away feeling as though they have all the answers.

◆ *Pack a punch with short stories.*

Just ask King David. He listened to a powerful short story told by a prophet named Nathan. The entire story, recorded in 2 Samuel 12:1-4, is four verses and less than 150 words long. But if you've ever read it, you realize that Nathan's brief story was life-changing for the most powerful man in all of Israel. (See the chapter on the Direct Spokesperson for more about this story.)

It should be illegal for a Christian communicator to bore an audience with the transforming message of Christ.

Creative storytelling doesn't always have to mean a narrative sermon that lasts for thirty minutes or even a lengthy tale that you spin for five minutes. Short stories injected in the right places can accomplish just as much, if not more.

For example, several months ago my father, my son (who was eight at the time), and I spoke at our church. My dad was to wrap up our comments by challenging people to pass on the baton of faith to the next generation. This is how he concluded:

"About twenty-five years ago, my wife and I returned from our first trip to the Holy Land. As we were taxiing up to the terminal, my wife's friend looked up at the airport windows and saw the people waiting to meet the flight. She exclaimed, 'Oh, look! All our children are here!'"

Then Dad tied the bow: "For parents, the one thing we all want to be able to say in heaven one day is 'Oh, look! All our children are here!'"

◆ *Don't neglect the role you play in becoming more creative.*

It should be illegal for a Christian communicator to bore an audience with the transforming message of Christ. You have a responsibility to share the good news with freshness. Mark Galli and Craig Brian Larson share a good reminder: "Certainly, our dependence on prayer and the inspiration of the Holy Spirit is the basis for our creativity, yet that does not nullify the human dimension. By our work habits and mind-set, we hinder or heighten inspiration."[15] Enhance your creativity by writing your material in different settings and at different times. You'll be surprised that such minor changes can cause creativity to flow rather than merely drip.

◆ *Avoid puffy sermons with no depth.*
Max Lucado warned Creative Storytellers to beware of superficial sermons. Make certain you put the time in on scriptural exposition. Listening by tape or the Internet to deep teachers and Bible scholars is, as Max suggested, a starting point for avoiding this weakness.

ENDNOTES

1 David A. Enyart, *Creative Anticipation: Narrative Sermon Designs for Telling the Story* (Philadelphia, PA: Xlibris Corporation, 2002), 69. See www.xlibris.com/Creative Anticipation.html.

2 Russ Blowers, comments (Indianapolis, IN: Castleton Rotary Club, 1988).

3 Clark Tanner, "High Quality Preaching Week In and Week Out" workshop (St. Louis, MO: North American Christian Convention, June 24, 1998).

4 Enyart, *Creative Anticipation: Narrative Sermon Designs for Telling the Story*, 25-26.

5 Paul S. Williams, *Laughter, Tears, and In-Between: Soulful Stories for the Journey* (Valley Forge, PA: Judson Press, 2001), ix.

6 Michael Duduit, ed., *Communicate with Power: Insights from America's Top Communicators* (Grand Rapids, MI: Baker Books, a division of Baker Book House Company, 1996), 141.

7 Williams, *Laughter, Tears, and In-Between: Soulful Stories for the Journey*, ix.

8 Incidentally, if you want to improve your skills in this area, read *Craddock Stories* by Fred B. Craddock (St. Louis, MO: Chalice Press, 2001) to learn from a pro.

9 Max added, "To be honest, I got that out of a movie. Tom Hanks says to Meg Ryan, 'I oh-so hope you will.' When I saw that, I thought, 'Ooh, that's strong.'"

10 Author's note: In nearly twenty years, Max has grown Oak Hills Church from a couple hundred to four thousand.

11 Fred Craddock, "Preaching Workshop #1" (Indianapolis, IN: North American Christian Convention, July 10, 2003).

12 Taken from HUMOR IN PREACHING by JOHN W. DRAKEFORD. Copyright © 1986 by John W. Drakeford. Used by permission of The Zondervan Corporation. Drakeford quotes Fant and Pinson, *Twenty Centuries of Great Preaching*.

13 Duduit, *Communicate with Power: Insights from America's Top Communicators*, 146-147.

14 Enyart, *Creative Anticipation: Narrative Sermon Designs for Telling the Story*, 138-139.

15 Taken from PREACHING THAT CONNECTS by CRAIG BRIAN LARSON; MARK GALLI. Copyright © 1994 by Mark Galli and Craig Brian Larson. Used by permission of The Zondervan Corporation.

CHAPTER **2**

The Direct Spokesperson

"When you know you're right, you don't care what others think. You know sooner or later it will come out in the wash."
—**Barbara McClintock**[1]

"Preach the Word; be prepared in season and out of season; correct, rebuke and encourage—with great patience and careful instruction. For the time will come when men will not put up with sound doctrine. Instead, to suit their own desires, they will gather around them a great number of teachers to say what their itching ears want to hear. They will turn their ears away from the truth and turn aside to myths." —**2 Timothy 4:2-4**

The Direct Spokesperson speaks to help people *decide* something.
The target is the listener's *will*.
Think Franklin Graham.

Similar styles: Revolutionary Leader, Cultural Prophet, Inspiring Orator

Words that describe this style: Firm, consistent, steady, clarion, unswerving, direct, reliable, forthright, politically incorrect

You might be a Direct Spokesperson if...
- it's music to your ears when someone says you "tell it like it is."
- the term *politically correct* isn't in your vocabulary.
- challenge and criticism roll off you like water off a duck's back.
- opposition *inspires* rather than *threatens* you.
- you seldom beat around the bush.

- on a regular basis your friends sarcastically say to you, "Tell us how you *really* feel!"
- you desire to cut through all the fluff and leave only the substance.

About This Style

Peter Cartwright, a nineteenth-century, circuit-riding Methodist preacher, was an uncompromising man. One Sunday morning before he was to preach, he was told that President Andrew Jackson was in the congregation. Officials warned Cartwright not to say anything out of line.

When he stood to preach, he said, "I understand that Andrew Jackson is here. I have been requested to be guarded in my remarks. Andrew Jackson will go to hell if he doesn't repent."

The congregation was shocked and wondered how the president would respond to his directness. After the service, President Jackson shook hands with Peter Cartwright and said, "Sir, if I had a regiment of men like you, I could whip the world."[2]

Teachers and preachers who are not concerned with approval ratings, popularity polls, and political correctness fall into this category.

Tell it like it is, and let the chips fall where they may—that sentiment aptly describes the Direct Spokesperson. Teachers and preachers who are not concerned with approval ratings, popularity polls, and political correctness fall into this category. You always know where they stand on an issue.

These individuals are focused on winning the world to Christ, and they feel called to sound that message regardless of the personal cost. Remember Peter's powerful stand before the Sanhedrin in Acts 5? The high priest reminded the apostles that they had been told not to teach in the name of Jesus. Peter replied, "We must obey God rather than men" (Acts 5:29).

Those words—"we must obey God rather than men"—convey the compulsion the Direct Spokesperson feels.

If you've ever attended a women's conference in a large arena or a Promise Keepers conference, you've no doubt heard this style. The frivolous is removed as the Direct Spokesperson boils down the message to its essence. Some may characterize these ladies and gentleman as calloused, but others understand that they strive for a simple and clear message.

The Engaging Humorist may try to win you over with humor, the Persuasive Motivator may appeal to your heart, but the hard-hitting Direct Spokesperson takes aim at your will. Her words may touch your heart, but that is secondary. Where others waffle on requesting a response, he dives in without hesitation. While other styles sometimes get lost in ambiguity, the Direct Spokesperson streamlines to convey a simple message in a simple manner. Cut out the fluff: Here are your choices—whose side are you on?

Matt Proctor delineates two similar styles: He says the Direct Spokesperson confronts our personal sin and challenges individuals to personal action, while the Cultural Prophet confronts cultural sin and challenges the church to corporate action.

This style also is a close relative to the Revolutionary Leader, but it tends to be a little more refined. Though neither the Revolutionary Leader nor the Direct Spokesperson is overly concerned about offending someone, the Direct Spokesperson's words are more calculated. Both are on a mission, but the Direct Spokesperson may invest more time in the verbal strategy.

The Apostle Paul was often a Direct Spokesperson. In every town he visited, he either started a riot or a revival—sometimes both! His direct challenge to Timothy was to "correct, rebuke and encourage" (2 Timothy 4:2).

The Old Testament prophet Nathan also was a Direct Spokesperson. In 2 Samuel 12, Nathan tells King David a short parable about a wealthy man who was loaded with sheep and cattle but still stole a poor neighbor's one little lamb. When the king pronounced judgment on the insensitive rich man's actions, Nathan moved in for the kill. The phrase *You are the man* no doubt echoed in David's mind for the rest of his life.

But Nathan didn't stop there. The prophet went on to clearly spell out the consequences of David's devious schemes.

Look at 2 Samuel 12:7-10:

Then Nathan said to David, "You are the man! This is what the Lord, the God of Israel, says: 'I anointed you king over Israel, and I delivered you from the hand of Saul. I gave your master's house to you, and your master's wives into your arms. I gave you the house of Israel and Judah. And if all this had been too little, I would have given you even more. Why did you despise the word of the Lord by doing what is evil in his eyes? You struck down Uriah the Hittite with the sword and took his wife to be your own. You killed him with the sword of the Ammonites. Now, therefore, the sword will never depart from your house, because you despised me and took the wife of Uriah the Hittite to be your own.'"

Please don't stereotype this communication style as caustic.

Nathan didn't say what King David's itching ears wanted to hear. Painful as it was, the prophet told David the truth. Note that the authority for being so direct was based on the truth that Nathan was sharing a word from the Lord. In the prophet's case, it had been revealed to him by God.

Please don't stereotype this communication style as caustic. People are longing for spiritual direction. They yearn for clear-cut instructions on how to head down the road that leads to God. Without compassionate directness, the masses will continue to flounder and remain lost. That's why the Direct Spokesperson loves Jesus' words in John 14:6: "I am the way and the truth and the life. No one comes to the Father except through me."

Give it a shot. Nothing ventured, nothing gained. Today's culture responds to brutal honesty rather than to backdoor, deceptive methods.

Jesus, a Direct Spokesperson

Throughout his ministry, Jesus consistently drove home simple, clear expectations. His message was not mired in the middle ground, and he conveyed clarity of purpose. Listen to these blunt statements that Jesus communicated to throngs of listeners:

• "If anyone comes to me and does not hate his father and mother, his wife and children, his brothers and sisters—yes, even his own life—he cannot be my disciple" (Luke 14:26). Jesus was using hyperbole to drive home just how intense our love for the Lord should be.

- "He will put the sheep on his right and the goats on his left" (Matthew 25:33). You are either a sheep or a goat. You are saved or lost. Jesus taught and loved people so that they could make the right choice.

- What about Christ's seven denunciations of the Pharisees in Matthew 23? "Woe to you, teachers of the law and Pharisees, you hypocrites!" (verse 13). That would qualify as being direct!

Franklin Graham, a Direct Spokesperson

Few have preached the gospel in person to millions of people. Our featured communicator for this chapter has—and quite effectively. To be known as Billy Graham's son would place quite a mantle of pressure on a guy. Franklin Graham has handled it well and has succeeded on his own. His clear-cut, compelling messages—coupled with his administrative abilities—allow him to lead crusades all around the world and head up a relief organization called Samaritan's Purse.

Franklin's sermons are characterized by a simple explanation of the gospel. He clearly presents the expectations for those who would accept the invitation to be followers of Christ. Characteristic of those who employ this style, he strives to please an audience of One.

Interview With Franklin Graham [3]

DAVE: When did you first realize that you had some gifts in communication?

FRANKLIN: Oh boy…I don't know. You know, when I took over the work of Samaritan's Purse, I remember talking to Bob Pierce. I said, "You know, Bob, you want me to take over Samaritan's Purse, but you go out and speak. You write the newsletters. I don't know how to do any of that. And Bob just looked at me, kind of smiled, and said, "God will show you." And you know, he's still showing me.

DAVE: You must be a fast learner because when you speak, you have a gift of being able to make it simple and clear. Who are some of the people who have influenced your communication style?

FRANKLIN: I've never tried to copy anybody. I've never listened to somebody and said, "Whoa, I want to do it that way." I'm not saying that's a bad thing to do, but I just haven't done it. In the past, I've watched people try to communicate by imitating somebody they look up to; it just doesn't work. The best thing is to speak and communicate in a way you're comfortable with. When you get outside of those comfortable boundaries, you don't communicate.

> I've watched people try to communicate by imitating somebody they look up to; it just doesn't work.

Whatever I want to say, I try and keep it short because people's attention spans are not as long as you might think! Sometimes we get behind the pulpit and think, "They're listening to every word I'm saying." They're not! I know because when I sit in their place, listening even to a great speaker, my mind drifts to this or that. So get into it quick, say what you've got to say, and shut up!

DAVE: No wonder I call your style the Direct Spokesperson! How long do you typically speak?

FRANKLIN: It depends. There have been times that I've preached in ten minutes. When you're speaking at an open-air meeting and you've got thunderstorms coming, you'd better get to the invitation as quickly as you can. Lightning is in the distance, and it's coming your way. You're not going to make it. So you learn to adapt. Normally I try to be to my invitation in about twenty, twenty-five minutes. The invitation itself could take as long as ten minutes, so my evangelistic messages are twenty-five minutes max.

> "Get into it quick, say what you've got to say, and shut up!"

DAVE: When you prepare a message, do you write out a manuscript or just an outline?

FRANKLIN: When speaking in a big stadium, I write out the message word-for-word and take it up with me. I don't follow it exactly, but sometimes a distraction or disturbance occurs in the audience. I'm talking about when somebody's trying to shout you down. At those times, you need something you can put your eyes on and go with. Instead of losing your train of thought or skipping something, you can read it word for word if you have to, just to get through it.

DAVE: Does that happen very often?

FRANKLIN: Sometimes, yeah. When you're preaching the gospel, the devil's not going to let you get up there and preach without trying to give you a bad day.

DAVE: I appreciate your boldness in spite of the hits you've taken due to your stand on the Bible. What is it that increases your boldness?

FRANKLIN: First of all, I have a dislike for people who try to be politically correct because I see them as compromisers. Even in the church now, we have a lot of people who want to be politically correct because they're trying to please men. The Bible makes very clear that we're not to please men. We're to try to please our Father in heaven. I think that's been my focus in my ministry: I want to please my Father in heaven. I'm a father, and I like it when someone speaks well of my children, you know. I think the Father likes it when we talk about Jesus and lift up Christ. So you can't go wrong with talking about Jesus, but a lot of people don't like that.

DAVE: What are some of your communication style's challenges that you've had to overcome? For example, Zig Ziglar says he'll work for four hours the night before giving a speech he's done a hundred times because he wants to refine it.

FRANKLIN: I'll do the same as Zig. I don't care how many times I've preached on a particular passage of Scripture, I'll spend several hours with it the day I preach it. If I'm going to speak that afternoon or evening, I'll take most of that day to work on the message—refining it, adding, deleting. You're always tweaking it; you're never satisfied with it.

> "I have a dislike for people who try to be politically correct because I see them as compromisers."

I also spend a lot of time just in prayer, realizing that this is God's gospel. It's not *my* message—it's *his* message. If I'm going to invite people to receive God's message—his invitation to his Son, Jesus Christ—I have to have his help.

To be successful when preaching an evangelistic message, you have to include the elements of the gospel: The fact that we've all sinned. God's love for you and perdition for sin. Jesus Christ—his death on the cross, his burial, his resurrection, that he's alive, that he's coming again. What our response is—that we've got to repent, confess our sins, be willing to turn from them, and by faith receive Christ into our lives. We've got to let him take control of our lives, our hearts, our minds. That has to be in every message. And don't complicate the message. Keep it so simple that a child can understand it. If a child can understand it, you know an adult can understand it.

"Don't complicate the message. Keep it so simple that a child can understand it."

DAVE: Don't you think that simplicity has been part of the reason people resonate with your preaching?

FRANKLIN: When Jesus spoke, he spoke in parables so that people could understand it. I mean, here's the Son of God who created the universe, created mankind. And yet he spoke at a level that children could understand. I just think we should do the same thing.

DAVE: Which comes more naturally for you—preparing for a message or delivering a message?

FRANKLIN: I enjoy the delivery. It's always hard to find the time for the discipline of preparation. During the preparation, I struggle with wanting to say this or that. I can't make up my mind sometimes. I literally have walked up to the pulpit and changed my message. Many times I have set my notes aside and given a completely different message because the one I'd prepared didn't feel right in my heart. I did that the Sunday before last.

DAVE: Do you ever ask ministry friends to read over a manuscript to see if you're going in the right direction?

FRANKLIN: No, I don't do that.

DAVE: Do you just speak based on your gut feeling for what the Lord's impressed upon your heart?

FRANKLIN: Yeah. Remember, this is God's gospel, and the Holy Spirit has to lead me. I'm always looking for illustrations, and people give me ideas and suggestions for illustrations. When it comes to the message, though, I don't seek other people's help.

DAVE: You do a great job of using Scripture in your lessons and sermons. Talk to me about how you plug Scripture into the life of your message.

FRANKLIN: There's no sense in giving the gospel message if you're not going to have a biblical basis. You start with a text, then you use different Scriptures to support the text you're preaching from. You have to include God's Word throughout your message to keep coming back to the authority.

I like to hold the Bible in the pulpit. When I say, "The Bible says…" it's in my hand. That's my authority—the authority for all of us as preachers. Now, some preachers today don't even take the Bible into the pulpit with them. They do everything on audio-visual, with the verses on a big screen. That's fine, but there's something about the image of the pastor holding the Word of God in his hand—the authority of the Scripture.

DAVE: Are there any disciplines you go through before you share God's Word?

FRANKLIN: Prayer, I think, is the number one thing I do in preparation. Secondly, I'll actually go into a room and quote Scripture or preach part of the sermon very loudly, just to exercise my voice. When you're speaking in a stadium, you're projecting hard even though you may have very good amplification because of the vastness of the place. If you don't exercise your voice, you're going to strain it.

DAVE: Describe your style of preaching in a few words.

FRANKLIN: I've never really thought about my style. People's styles change. When my father was preaching back in the early to late '40s, he would prance from one side of the stage to the other. He would point, and he would quote Scriptures one right after another—very dramatic. His style in the '70s was a lot different. And it's different today.

One thing I always try to do is be excited about the message. I don't want to come across as though I'm thinking, "Oh, I really don't want to do this tonight." When you get up there, you want to speak with authority. Not that you're jumping around, but that there's a passion. You're not just *saying* words, but you truly *believe* them!

DAVE: Is it difficult to keep that passion all the time?

FRANKLIN: There are days when you don't feel good. There are days when you're tired. There are days when you're facing pressures at home. The devil does this to you. That's why before I get up to speak, I pray.

I pray, "God, you help me. This is your gospel. This is your message. I cannot do this apart from you. And so as I stand up there to deliver your gospel and extend your invitation, I commit myself to you. I rededicate myself to you. Fill me now with your Holy Spirit power."

I've found that I have to do that every time. And then when I get up there, all the pressures and tensions disappear.

"You cannot speak this gospel message without getting shots from everybody."

DAVE: I know you've received all kinds of resistance from the prince of darkness because you are direct and committed to God's Word.

FRANKLIN: We all have adversity. I don't think I've had more than anybody else. It just comes in different forms. The devil doesn't let us rest. And you cannot speak this gospel message without getting shots from everybody. You expect the shots from the liberal press or those in the media who are lost. But then you also take shots from within the household of faith, from other Christians. The devil's not going to let you rest, so don't fight back. God hasn't called me to fight these people. I just proclaim the gospel. I proclaim the truth. When they throw stones at me, I just smile and go on.

Make no mistake—Franklin is frank. There's a reason his candid messages are shorter than yours or mine: He doesn't mince words. Millions resonate with the direct, honest message Franklin preaches because he speaks the truth *and* does so in love.

Advice on Refining This Style
◆ *Rely on God's authority—not your own!*
Respected preacher Haddon W. Robinson warns communicators about losing credibility by neglecting the source of authority. He

writes, "The constant temptation of the preacher is to cry out some other message than the Scriptures—a political system, a theory of economics, a new religious philosophy. No matter that this may be done in authoritative tones, if a preacher does not preach the Scriptures he abandons his authority. He no longer confronts men or women with the Word of God but simply speaks another word from a man."[4]

We don't need another word from a man or woman. For preachers or teachers, God's Word is the authority. The Holy Spirit may impress something upon you during your quiet time, or the still, small voice of the Lord may speak through the words of a Christian friend. Regardless of the method, the authority for directness is the Word of God or a word from God.

The Bible itself promises that "all men are like grass, and all their glory is like the flowers of the field; the grass withers and the flowers fall, but the word of the Lord stands forever" (1 Peter 1:24-25). How dare we think that we can be Direct Spokespersons if the only things we pass on come from human origin and our own limited thinking?

◆ Lay the groundwork for your directness.

While there is power in being direct, your strength becomes a weakness if you haven't prepared your class or congregation to receive the message. If you don't set the stage with supporting Scriptures and logic, the directness and the impact of your communication will be diluted. Don't give people an excuse to misinterpret your directness as abruptness. Prepare them so your message leads to life change.

◆ Share the whole story.

There's a tendency to think of directness as negative. But the most effective Christian leaders are skilled at positively expressing the clear-cut benefits of the Christian life. It's true that they warn against the consequences of a life without the Lord, but they balance it with the blessings for the committed believer.

I'm reminded of a statement made by Dr. J. Henry Jowett

during the Yale Convention of 1912. He said, "The very term 'good news' implies that there is such a thing as bad news, the very proclamation of salvation presupposes a state of being lost. Hell is the dark background on which the brilliant picture of the gospel is painted. But without the background, you have no picture."[5]

◆ *Speak the truth in love.*

The ministerial staff at Southeast Christian Church used to have an annual four-day staff retreat. The highlight of our time together (next to the afternoon recreation!) was a hard-hitting challenge from Bob Russell, our senior minister. We didn't feel like the retreat was complete until Bob laid it on the line. He never minced words concerning his expectations for staff in the areas of integrity, work ethic, and doctrinal purity. His directness always served as a catalyst for spiritual renewal and vocational inspiration. But if we didn't know he cared about each of us, that message may have sounded like a dentist's drill rather than a loving warning.

This style is best utilized when it's tempered with compassion.

This style is best utilized when it's tempered with compassion. The Direct Spokesperson who conveys genuine concern and joy will be effective. But in time, those who view the pulpit as a fort from which to hurl verbal artillery will run out of ammunition.

Bob Russell sums up the goal for all Christian communicators when he says, "Truth without love is dogmatism. Love without truth is sentimentality. Speaking the truth in love is Christianity."[6]

◆ *Keep it simple.*

Think back to a couple of statements in Franklin Graham's interview:

"So get into it quick, say what you've got to say, and shut up!"

"Don't complicate the message. Keep it so simple that a child can understand it. If a child can understand it, you know an adult can understand it."

The Direct Spokesperson is most effective when the flow of the compelling address is effortless. Simplicity and focus serve both the listener and the speaker.

◆ Avoid the "like it or lump it" approach.

In your effort to be direct, be certain you don't come across as cavalier or uncaring to those who aren't quite ready to accept your invitation to commit to Christ and his lordship. While Direct Spokespersons aren't concerned with whether their words enhance or detract from their own popularity, they should still have some tact.

◆ Expect flack, but don't feel compelled to fight back.

Jesus said, "Woe to you when all men speak well of you" (Luke 6:26). Don't be surprised when your directness is criticized. The key is to evaluate the criticism, along with your own spirit and heart. Remember Franklin Graham's words: "God hasn't called me to fight these people."

Or, as someone once said, "Never get into a spitting contest with a skunk. Even if you win, you'll come out smelling bad."

ENDNOTES

1 Claudia Wallis, "Honoring a Modern Mendel," Time (October 24, 1983), 54.

2 Dave Kennedy, sermon (Clarksville, IN: Eastside Christian Church, January 1998).

3 Travel schedules precluded Franklin Graham and me from meeting in person, so this is the only interview in the book that was conducted by telephone.

4 Haddon W. Robinson, *Making a Difference in Preaching* (Grand Rapids, MI: Baker Books, a division of Baker Book House Company, 1999), 63.

5 Dave Stone, *I'd Rather See a Sermon: Showing Your Friends the Way to Heaven* (Joplin, MO: College Press Publishing Co., 1996), 118-119.

6 Bob Russell, *When God Builds a Church: 10 Principles for Growing a Dynamic Church* (West Monroe, LA: Howard Publishing Co., Inc., 2000), 13.

CHAPTER 3

The Scholarly Analytic

"Several years ago, I saw the prolific Ray Bradbury interviewed on PBS. Dick Cavett posed the question I longed to ask: How do you produce such massive quantities of good stuff? Bradbury replied, 'The more you put into your head, the more you can get out.'" —P e t e r L e s c h a k[1]

"Anyone who lives on milk, being still an infant, is not acquainted with the teaching about righteousness. But solid food is for the mature, who by constant use have trained themselves to distinguish good from evil. Therefore let us leave the elementary teachings about Christ and go on to maturity, not laying again the foundation of repentance from acts that lead to death, and of faith in God, instruction about baptisms, the laying on of hands, the resurrection of the dead, and eternal judgment. And God permitting, we will do so."
—H e b r e w s 5 : 1 3 – 6 : 3

The Scholarly Analytic speaks to help people *understand* something. The target is the listener's *logic*.

Think Tim Keller.

Similar styles: Cultural Prophet, Passionate Teacher, Convincing Apologist

Words that describe this style: Educated, cultured, organized, intellectual, well-schooled, trained, logical, systematic, academic, reasoned, learned, studious

You might be a Scholarly Analytic if...

• you outline extensively before you begin writing a message or presentation.

- your manuscripts are meticulously driven by outlines (form even overrules function).
- people you're conversing with frequently say, "I have absolutely no idea what in the world you are talking about."
- people listen to you and respect what you say because of your scholarship and knowledge.
- you view word studies as a recreational activity rather than as work.
- your IQ is higher than the score of an average bowler or a lousy golfer.

About This Style

When Josh McDowell was in college, he considered himself an agnostic. While there, however, he encountered a group of Christian students and professors who stood out on campus. They exuded confidence and conviction. McDowell made their acquaintance.

Within two weeks he found himself talking with some members of the group, and the topic turned to God. McDowell balked, thinking that Christianity was only for the weak-minded. But his new friends challenged him to objectively examine the evidence of Jesus' claim to be the Son of God. McDowell recalls, "I thought it was a joke. I thought, *How could something as flimsy as Christianity stand up to an intellectual examination?*"

Josh accepted their challenge and spent several months researching Scripture, trying to prove that Christ's claim was untrue. McDowell thought if he could prove that the Bible was unreliable, then Christians would have nothing to support their claims. Though Christians could prove that Scripture taught of Christ's miraculous birth, healings, and even his resurrection, McDowell was out to prove that the Scriptures were simply a myth and fable.

McDowell writes:

My research became more and more intense... And after months of examining historical evidences, I came to one conclusion: If I were to remain intellectually honest, I had to admit that the Old and New Testament documents were the most reliable writings of all antiquity! And that brought me face-to-face with the claims of Christ...

You see, the historical evidence convinced my mind that the Jesus who lived two thousand years ago had to be the one true God. But it was his love that gripped my heart and compelled me to commit my life to Christ.[2]

Scholarly Analytics are responsible for stretching the minds of so many listeners. They aim their arrows at listeners' logic, challenging them with wisdom, information, and organization.

Some of your favorite teachers and preachers are probably Scholarly Analytics. They have incredible gifts: They can outline and balance a sermon or lesson in their sleep, and they can converse about topics as diverse as your mind can conceive.

It may seem strange to lump the scholar with the analytic, but observation and experience show that people who are wired to think with their left brain often are both. The scholar is studious, and the analytic carefully organizes ideas.

If you're a Scholarly Analytic, your study and preparation show. You wouldn't think of standing in front of people unless you'd done your homework and put your thoughts into some semblance of order. This organization comes in handy when sifting through all that swims through your brain. You may even enjoy the preparation process more than the delivery.

Scholarly analytics can influence the influencers.

Consider for a minute the opportunities this style presents to one who speaks for a living. Scholarly Analytics can influence the influencers. Their education, knowledge, organization, and academic achievement cause the cerebral seekers to sit up and listen. Those pensive listeners who need to be totally convinced about every detail of faith before they make a commitment may take longer to reach, but they tend to stick once they've made the commitment.

I'm not very comfortable with this style, but it's important for me to integrate some scholarly thinking and analytical planning into my speaking. In my audience (and yours) are people who are wired differently from me. They're not amused by my Barney Fife imitation, but they take notice when I quote G. K. Chesterton; only then, in their minds, have I earned the right to be heard.

I took my daughters with me on a business trip to San Antonio, Texas. As always, the things that stand out to children on a long distance excursion are quite different from what we adults remember. Unfortunately, our time did not allow for any visits to historical sites. When we returned home to Kentucky, my eight-year-old, Sadie, was excitedly telling her Uncle Paul all about the trip. Being a history buff, Paul was quick to ask, "Sadie, did you get to see the Alamo?"

With enthusiasm, Sadie innocently replied, "Yeah, we rented our car from there!"

Sadie missed out on the history. That scenario wouldn't happen in a church led by a Scholarly Analytic. Some Christian leaders and teachers may fail to prepare. As they lead a Bible study or expound to a congregation, they unknowingly miss out on the historical and spiritual implications of the very passages they are illuminating.

While this has been a difficult chapter for me to write, doing so has spurred more personal growth than has writing about the other styles. I need to grow in this style. I desperately need this style's wisdom and organization. Maybe you're like me, and your ministry responsibilities have forced you to dig more deeply during your preparation. This chapter either will reinforce your natural style or will stretch you—and me—out of our comfort zones.

Jesus, a Scholarly Analytic

Christ had the knowledge and wisdom of the Scholarly Analytic, turning heads with his understanding even at the tender age of twelve (Luke 2:42-47). Later in his earthly ministry, the crowds were amazed at his teaching. Do you remember why their jaws dropped when he spoke? Matthew 7:29 says it was "because he taught as one who had authority, and not as their teachers of the law."

Jesus revealed the source of his teaching in John 7:16: "My

teaching is not my own. It comes from him who sent me." Through studying and preparation, the hallmarks of the Scholarly Analytic, we can follow in the footsteps of the Master.

Tim Keller, a Scholarly Analytic

The featured Scholarly Analytic is an outgoing, humorous gentleman from New York City. Not only does he typify this style, but he also happens to minister in a cosmopolitan area where this style is almost a must. Tim Keller felt the Lord calling him from the scholarly task of teaching at Westminster Theological Seminary to start a church in New York City. It's grown from a handful of people to more than four thousand in attendance.

Surrounded by high-rise buildings in downtown Manhattan on Madison Avenue, Tim has found that people in the Big Apple have to be impressed by your intellect or they'll never come back to a service. Tim has a great gift of breaking down concepts. A friend of mine from New York described his style with these words: "He's one of the few intellectuals who is able to put things on the bottom shelf where you can reach them."

Interview With Tim Keller

DAVE: When did you first realize you had a gift of communication?

TIM: It was pretty slow to dawn on me. I had a church in Virginia for nine years, where I served blue-collar people, simple people, very great people. However, in a smaller town, your *pastoring* sets up your preaching. People decide whether you're wise by whether you love them. If they decide you're wise because of the way you counsel them and because you love them, then they'll listen to your preaching and say, "That was good. That helped me."

Then when I went to Westminster Seminary, I taught preaching and ministry. While I was there, I spoke several times for a large church, Tenth Presbyterian. That was the first time I noticed that people responded strongly to my preaching. Before that I would have thought of myself as a little too intellectual for most people—more of a teacher than a preacher. But there, it hit me.

So I was in the ministry for more than a decade before I realized I was pretty good at communicating.

DAVE: Your insight into rural and city churches is fascinating.

TIM: In a big city or suburb, the professionals want to know whether you've "got it" in the pulpit. If, in their minds, you're a great preacher, then they'll let you talk to them about their problems. There, your *preaching* sets up your pastoring. It's totally the opposite from a rural church.

"You can quote Sartre and Camus and still be kind of dynamic."

To take it further, your preaching also sets up your leadership in those settings. People will listen to you and let you pastor them, but they'll also listen to you as a visionary. Here at Redeemer Presbyterian, I've got to concentrate on preaching because preaching runs the engine of a big city church. I have to make it the priority as I never have before.

DAVE: Do any people, past or present, who have influenced your communication style come to mind?

TIM: Early on it was R.C. Sproul. He showed that it's OK to be academic and intellectual. You can quote Sartre and Camus and still be kind of dynamic. Realizing that was actually a very important first layer.

I think the second layer would be when I got here. I was desperately asking, "How do you preach evangelistically all the time without it sounding like the same old thing?" I realized that it is much easier to get non-Christians to come to church in a city than it is in a suburb. But I had to learn from Europeans because New York is much more like Europe than it is the rest of America.

So I got hold of Dr. David Martyn Lloyd-Jones' evening sermons, which were directed to non-Christians. Evidently, his morning service had about one thousand people—mostly his congregation members—but his evening service had about two thousand people from all over London. These people were Christians who would bring their friends to hear the doctor because he was intellectual. In the evenings, he would quote the newspaper. He would quote socialists. He would do different things, but he was very expository. He really got into the text. And he never bored you; he came at you from some different direction.

He always started from a text, and he preached evangelistically from that text—even Old Testament texts, even Jeremiah. It just was remarkable to me. Those sermons had a big impact on me.

I also listened to Dick Lucas, who also had a church in downtown London and a very evangelistic Tuesday service for business types.

DAVE: How does preaching in New York City differ from preaching in other places?

TIM: New York is sort of like a big college campus on steroids! New Yorkers are so gregarious and opinionated, and everybody wants to debate you. At the end of every service, people came up to me—half of whom weren't Christians—and told me right away what they liked and didn't like. That would never really happen in Virginia—or most anywhere else. New Yorkers aren't intimidated. They aren't afraid. They're rude. And they had no trouble telling me about it. Probably twenty people a week just wanted to talk to me about the sermon. That's just the way they are. I got so much positive reinforcement for the things that clicked, but I never went back again to the things that either confused or mystified people.

I learned an awful lot when I first got here. One unique thing about Redeemer Presbyterian is that about 75 percent of the four thousand people who come each week are single. So first, it's vastly easier to get a non-Christian single person to church because singles make unilateral decisions. Second, Christian singles have non-Christian single friends who are a lot closer to them than are Christian families with their non-Christian family friends. So it's natural for singles to invite these close friends to church.

Also, cities are places of stress. People are on edge, they have a lot of questions, they're in turmoil, they're always moving, they're always changing. Therefore, there are far more spiritual questions.

DAVE: How do those circumstances affect your communication?

TIM: I have to preach a sermon that makes Christians who come say, "I wish my non-Christian friend could hear this." That's the key. Christians come and hear a sermon that doesn't just edify them, but also makes them say, "That's what I've been trying to say to my non-Christian friend, and I haven't been doing a very good job of it. Besides, the music and everything was so interesting that it would blow my friend's mind. They have such a negative view of Christianity, and this will be interesting. I want to bring my friend."

"I have to preach a sermon that makes Christians who come say, 'I wish my non-Christian friend could hear this.'"

DAVE: Every communication style has a down side. What are some weaknesses associated with being a Scholarly Analytic, and how do you overcome them?

TIM: Well, I'm not sure I'm trying to overcome them. I think I'm living with them! I've never had a "normal" church. I had a church where a lot of people couldn't read and write, and now I have a church where an M.B.A. from Harvard is like a green card! So you struggle to make sure you're as diverse a communicator as possible.

Here, you've got a bunch of people who are utterly neglected—the high achievers, highly educated, highly sophisticated people. In other settings, you don't have enough of them to dedicate a full preaching style to them. But here, there are plenty to fill four services!

On the other hand, a lot of people find the style too esoteric. I mean, I think I'm pretty down-to-earth. I'm pretty good at making theological and philosophical concepts graspable. But there's a limit. So of course some people come and say, "This is just over my head."

In an urban setting, you usually fit certain personas. One of them is the Activist. One of them is the Artist. One of them is the Professor. One of them is the Dealmaker. I thought, "OK, I'm not a Dealmaker. I'm not really an Activist. I'm a little bit of an Artist. I'm basically a Professor, so let's just do it."

From there, authenticity is a big deal because we have a lot of young people. I think one of the reasons I've appealed to that age group is that, as much as possible, I'm trying to just speak out of my heart.

DAVE: Do you manuscript?

TIM: It's kind of a manuscript. It's my own shorthand. It's two or three small pages that I read over a few times before the sermon. I don't practice out loud—just in my mind—but it takes just as long. While I'm preaching, I never look at those pages. If I don't memorize it, it really looks stilted.

DAVE: When you preach, you paint some vivid word pictures.

TIM: You do have to use imagery. I got that from Jonathan Edwards. Edwards believed very, very much in sense appeal.

One discipline I have to employ to overcome my weaknesses is rewriting. When I first put something down on paper, it seems like every idea has to be there. I probably need four rewrites, or it will be way too long.

DAVE: Talk about your reading habits.

TIM: That's key: I read a lot more than most people. I read a lot of magazines, and I read across the spectrum. So I read The New Yorker from cover to cover, but I also read The Nation, which is a socialist magazine—angry left-wing. I read the Utne Reader, which is New Age, happy-clappy reading.

As I read across the spectrum, I argue in my mind with the writers. I write things down all the time as I argue, and that's really where the ideas come from.

DAVE: Which is easier for you—the preparation or the delivery?

TIM: The delivery.

DAVE: Does that come out of your being an extrovert?

TIM: Well, I do like to be "out there." But the preparation just seems to come so slowly. I'm quite a perfectionist, which means I do not let myself finish the preparation quickly. I always force myself to go longer than I'd like to. I'm constantly critiquing as I'm writing. But when I'm out there preaching, I can pull it together without much trouble. So I feel much happier when I deliver than when I'm writing.

DAVE: Your outlining skills are superb.

TIM: I type my message in outline form, all the way down to the A-B and 1-2. That helps me keep track of where I am.

DAVE: Have you always been like that, or did you take some steps to strengthen that?

TIM: I taught preaching at Westminster Seminary and listened to a lot of sermons. Many times I couldn't tell where people were going, and I get very impatient with that. Outlining helps me say,

"Outlining helps me say, 'I want you to realize where we're going and how we're going to get there.'" "I want you to realize where we're going and how we're going to get there." People are more patient then because they know where in the sermon you are.

You can do this even when you create a problem—my wife, Kathy, calls it "pulling a rabbit out of the hat." In most cases, the best sermons create a problem and then solve it with Jesus and the gospel. Nevertheless, there's still got to be an outline. So sometimes I outline a message that "takes the rabbit out of the hat." Listeners feel like there's no way out...there's no way out...but then Jesus becomes the way out.

Each of the styles in this book has strengths to accentuate and weaknesses to improve. The Scholarly Analytic is no exception. The ability to share truths from biblical knowledge and scholarship in understandable fashion is a dream come true for a Christian communicator. Tim has succeeded because he works hard to keep his intellectualism a strength and goes to great lengths to keep it from becoming a barrier. He relates to the sophisticated in New York City while still conveying an approachability to his listeners.

Advice on Refining This Style
◆ *Use this style to open doors.*
Very few of the communication styles in this book would get a speaker an audience with both a king and a governor. The Apostle Paul was a natural Scholarly Analytic, though, and he *was* allowed such an audience (Acts 26).

A Direct Spokesperson or Revolutionary Leader wouldn't have been given a chance for fear of a revolt or embarrassing challenge. (Just imagine what the tabloids did, years before, when John the Baptist challenged Herod for marrying his sister-in-law!) An Engaging Humorist wouldn't have been given a chance either; the king already had court jesters, and even a freed prisoner would have had to work his way through the Jerusalem stand-up scene before landing the prestigious "Tribute to the King" gig.

But being an intellectual Pharisee in a previous life had its advantages! Paul, not your run-of-the-mill prisoner, probably garnered some respect and carried some clout. This apostle was eloquent, informed, well-read, and intellectually stimulating. Paul's brilliant mind connected with the educated aristocracy and earned him a right to be heard.

◆ *Avoid constant intellectual insights.*

While a handful of listeners would enjoy and connect with constant deep truths and explanations, you'll lose the rest. It's better to reach out to all, but you can use this style intermittently to include a challenging, cerebral teaching. That way everyone can remain "with you"—and you have earned the right to be heard by the intellectual listener.

◆ *See the Bible as a life-giving love letter from God, not as some textbook.*

If your study of the Bible is merely for the head, then you're missing something. The heart is the source of life, while the mind is the storehouse for knowledge. Sometimes put the pen and highlighter to the side, and just allow the Word to speak to your heart. As you study and dig and delve, let the Scriptures change *you* along with your listeners.

> While a handful of listeners would enjoy and connect with constant deep truths and explanations, you'll lose the rest.

◆ *Research + transparency = communication.*

You may be extremely intelligent and able to explain the historical and spiritual implications of any Bible story, but you'll never connect with your audience if you don't humbly admit weakness. The most effective Scholarly Analytics are approachable, practical, and vulnerable. While they may "have all the answers," their attitude doesn't communicate that. People want to be near them and listen to them because they convey authenticity rather than simply knowledge.

George Barna says listeners "want somebody who is realistic, who is vulnerable, who is struggling, and who is saying, 'I have not mastered it, but this is where I am at this point in time. I think this is a useful strategy or perspective. I don't have it totally together; grow with me.'"[3]

◆ Read across the spectrum.

If you want to grow as a Scholarly Analytic, you'll have to draw your teaching material from a deeper well. Read aggressively from a variety of perspectives, as Tim Keller suggested. Takes notes in the margins, and flag pages with sticky notes to use later. Transfer any thoughts, ideas, or quotes to your computer so you'll always have them at your disposal.

◆ Use outlines to stimulate rather than to limit.

Scholarly Analytics tend to be organized, and that often means they use outlines. While some people may see outlines as a limitation, they also can spark creativity. Peter Leschak writes, "Limits—that is, form—challenge the mind, forcing creativity. Let's say I wish to express romantic love. I could write a sloppy, gushy love note, but my effort would be better spent if I wrote a love sonnet. As soon as I decide to produce a sonnet, I'm restricted to 14 lines, a specific rhyme scheme and meter. In the process of trying to fit my feelings and ideas into this form, I'll end up exploring avenues and notions that would never have emerged from a simple, undemanding note…The more you limit yourself, the more you set yourself free."[4]

On the other hand, realize that outlines may help *you* more than they help your listeners. While outlines may be cute, witty, or alliterative, they rarely lead people to salvation. Strike that—they *never* lead people to salvation. In twenty years of preaching, I've never seen a person come forward in tears during the invitation and say, "When the final point of your sermon began with an R, just like the other points did, I knew it was time to give my heart to Jesus."

If such a thing ever did happen, I would probably say, "Thanks for Responding."

Don't misunderstand me. Your analytical skills can serve as a vehicle to make the message compelling. Your expert delineation can remove distractions and create a seamless flow. But as you establish an outline, make certain you put your emphasis on filling it in with meaningful material.

◆ *Make genuine understanding your goal.*
I read in Reader's Digest about a three-and-a-half-year-old boy who was sitting with his father eating an apple. After several bites the boy asked, "Daddy, why is my apple turning brown?"

His father answered, "Because after you ate the skin off, the meat of the apple came into contact with the air which caused it to oxidize thus changing its molecular structure and turning it into a different color."

I love the boy's response. After a lengthy pause, the son asked, "Daddy, are you talking to me?"[5]

The Scholarly Analytic's success is in direct correlation to how well he or she enhances the listeners' understanding. The point is not for listeners to memorize facts or statistics, but to help them take away a new, integrated understanding of the material.

After reading my thoughts for this chapter, preaching professor Matt Proctor observed a distinction between the Scholarly Analytic and the Passionate Teacher. He said, "The teacher puts new facts into a person's head, while the analytic helps people understand the relationship among those facts."

The point is not for listeners to memorize facts or statistics, but to help them take away a new, integrated understanding of the material.

◆ *Find ways to be fresh and interesting.*
During my interview with featured Cultural Prophet Charles Colson, he spoke of a theologian who was incredibly intellectual and scholarly. This man of vast knowledge was still able to teach the Bible in fresh, practical terms. His secret was to occasionally teach a class of youngsters, which drove him to explain deep spiritual truths in simple and clear terms.

What wisdom! You could ask some of your trusted listeners to honestly evaluate how fresh your methods are. Read periodicals you normally don't read. Gather ideas and input from people who are older and younger than you. Use vivid imagery in order to balance the heavy, scholastic material you're naturally drawn to. Utilize different approaches—transform intellectual material into a "rap," for example, and deliver it with a band backing you up. (Perhaps not!) I tried that approach—once—and the congregation was so surprised that they gave me a standing ovation.

Word choices should be made for practicality purposes—not to impress.

◆ *Allow your intellect to attract, not deter.*

Some seem to use their superior knowledge as a belittling weapon. Those communicators turn off the majority of their audiences and reduce their targets to small groups. An air of arrogance does not hold people's attention. Word choices should be made for practicality purposes—not to impress.

Erwin McManus, the featured Revolutionary Leader, also warns against arrogance in preaching. Erwin is extremely intelligent, cultured, and well-read, so his words are self-directed. He says: "I spent ten years working with people who had a third-grade education. Ten years working among the poor. I had a philosophical, theological background. My wife would say to me, 'Who were you talking to? No one understood you!'

"I felt like I was going through this sandpaper where God was stripping away from me all the arrogance and all my desire to look smart, all the desire to communicate things at a level that would impress people. Jesus was the smartest guy who ever lived, and yet his language was intelligible to anyone. I have no toleration for preaching that goes above people's heads because then you are preaching for yourself.

◆ *Respond to your audience.*

Everyone is different. Listeners have their own passions and interests. If you go too deep with your gleanings, you may drown your audience in boredom. If the truth or expectation isn't clear to them, they won't follow through. I've heard that Howard

Hendricks used to teach seminary students, "If it's a mist in the pulpit, it's a fog in the pew!"[6]

Haddon Robinson, a teacher of preachers, tells of a time his scholarly efforts backfired:

> Five minutes into the sermon...I knew I was in trouble. The people weren't with me. At the ten-minute mark, people were falling asleep. One man sitting near the front began to snore. Worse, he didn't disturb anyone! No one was listening...The problem was that I spent the whole sermon wrestling with the tough theological issues, issues that intrigued me...I didn't speak to the life questions of my audience. I answered my questions, not theirs. Some of the men and women I spoke to that day were close to going home to be with the Lord. What they wanted to know was, "Will he toss me into some ditch of a grave, or will he take me safely home to the other side?"...They wanted to hear me say..."God only spent six days creating the world, and look at its beauty! Imagine, then, what the home he has been preparing for you must be like. When you come to the end of this life, that's what he'll have waiting for you." That's what I should have preached.[7]

ENDNOTES

1 Peter Leschak, "The Five-Step Creativity Workout," Writer's Digest (November 1991), 28.

2 Josh McDowell & Bob Hostetler, *Beyond Belief to Convictions* (Carol Stream, IL: Tyndale House Publishers, 2002), 38-40.

3 Michael Duduit, *Communicate with Power: Insights from America's Top Communicators* (Grand Rapids, MI: Baker Books, a division of Baker Book House Company, 1996), 23-24.

4 Leschak, "The Five-Step Creativity Workout," 27.

5 Stuart Cooke, contribution (Reader's Digest, December 1988), 93.

6 Andy Stanley, comments (Atlanta, GA: Catalyst Conference, 2002).

7 Haddon W. Robinson, *Making a Difference in Preaching* (Grand Rapids, MI: Baker Books, a division of Baker Book House Company, 1999), 85-86.

CHAPTER **4**

The Revolutionary Leader

"A leader is someone who is able to take you to a place you never would have gone on your own." —**Joel Barker**[1]

"But if I say, 'I will not mention him or speak any more in his name,' his word is in my heart like a fire, a fire shut up in my bones. I am weary of holding it in; indeed, I cannot."
—**Jeremiah 20:9**

The Revolutionary Leader speaks to help people *ignite* something.
The target is the listener's *passion*.
Think Erwin McManus.

Similar styles: Direct Spokesperson, Passionate Teacher, Persuasive Motivator, Unorthodox Artist

Words that describe this style: Intense, bold, challenging, brave, audacious, daring, courageous, renegade, take-charge, valiant, maverick

You might be a Revolutionary Leader if...
- your words can cause adrenaline surges and an increase in your listeners' blood pressure.
- you inspire applause or verbal affirmation because audience or class members feel like they'll explode if they don't validate what you're saying.
- you're sickened by Christian leaders who "just do church" and never try to impact their community for Christ.
- your philosophy is to ask forgiveness rather than permission, especially when speaking about a controversial topic.

- you resonate with the phrase "I'd rather burn out than rust out."
- you see a plaguing problem or a crisis in the church as an opportunity to spiritually lead the necessary transformation.
- you almost enjoy stepping on toes at times.

About This Style

Tony Campolo, sociology professor at Eastern University and popular speaker, enjoys telling about a women's conference he addressed. The women were being challenged with a several-thousand-dollar goal for their mission projects. The event chairperson turned to Campolo and asked if he would pray for God's blessing upon the women as they considered what they might give to achieve the goal. To her utter surprise, Campolo graciously declined her invitation by saying, "I won't pray for this need because you already have the resources necessary to complete this mission project right here in this room."

The chairperson nervously said, "Bravo, bravo! We get your point, Dr. Campolo."

Campolo took the microphone again and, in his typical fashion, said, "No, I don't think you do."

He continued, "It would be inappropriate to ask for God's blessing when God has already blessed you with the abundance and means to achieve this goal. The necessary gifts are in your hands. As soon as we take an offering and underwrite this mission project, I will be glad to thank God for freeing us to be the generous, responsible, and accountable stewards we are called to be as Christian disciples."

When these individuals communicate, they move listeners toward life change.

The ladies emptied their purses and brought their money to the front. Even the chairperson gave what she had in her billfold. The offering was quickly counted, and they found that they had exceeded the goal. Campolo then led a joyous prayer of thanksgiving for God's abundant blessings and for the faithful stewardship of God's people. His prayer was met with a huge ovation—even the woman in charge clapped.[2]

Certain individuals were born to lead. When these individuals communicate, they move listeners toward life change. I call them

Revolutionary Leaders.

As you read this chapter, names and faces will come to mind—people who communicate in a way that challenges spectators to become participants. Listening to Revolutionary Leaders is reminiscent of the coach's talk in the locker room prior to the game; when it's over, you're pumped and ready to take on anyone or anything in your path.

These communicators bring about change more quickly than the other styles; in doing so, they may not rack up points on the "tact-meter." But Revolutionary Leaders will endure complaints by Christians offended by their forthrightness in order to see several people commit their lives to Christ. If this is your primary style, an intensity oozes out of you as you speak.

This communication style does *not* work well in a church or organization that's satisfied with where it is.

When preparing sermons or lessons, Revolutionary Leaders are guided by this burning question: "How can I *make* these people *want* to change?" This is slightly different from Persuasive Motivators, who are guided by the question "How can I *help* these people change?" The Revolutionary Leader also is similar to the Convincing Apologist. The difference is that the latter is more apt to touch you intellectually, while the former will touch you emotionally.

Circumstances in the community or country sometimes dictate a need for revolutionary leadership. Perhaps you're attempting to unite unbelievers with the message of salvation. Perhaps you want different factions within the church to think together with a kingdom consciousness rather than debating their favorite music style or carpet color. Strong leadership is necessary for the church to grow spiritually and numerically. This communication style does *not* work well in a church or organization that's satisfied with where it is. Such cases become an exercise in pulling teeth, which is never fun—even with the Novocain.

The Revolutionary Leader is a pretty common style for Christian leaders, simply because most who pursue teaching, directing, or preaching have a propensity toward leading groups of people. Other Christian leaders need to forsake the ministry of mediocrity and the climate of complacency by experimenting with the intensity of a revolutionary. I've heard Tony Campolo say, "Instead of praying, 'If I should die before I wake'...maybe we should be praying, 'If I should wake before I die!'"[3]

If leadership is not your gift, then this style probably isn't your natural strong suit. Not every communicator's heart beats faster when discussing the topic of leadership. That's OK, but I hope and pray this chapter prompts you to dabble with this style. I'm not suggesting a drastic overnight makeover of your normal communication methods, but why not take the bull by the horns and strive to rally the troops? If you do, you may find that God is using you to start a positive uprising in your congregation or class.

Jesus, a Revolutionary Leader

Throughout Christ's ministry, he made revolutionary comments on a regular basis. Listen to some of his statements:

• "I and the Father are one" (John 10:30).
• "Destroy this temple, and I will raise it again in three days" (John 2:19).
• "I am the resurrection and the life. He who believes in me will live, even though he dies" (John 11:25).

He began his revolution with perhaps the most powerful statement he ever made: "Follow me."

Wow! Is it any wonder that Jesus' message and manner started a revolution that is still on the move today?

Erwin McManus, a Revolutionary Leader

The term "Revolutionary Leader" is the perfect description for this chapter's featured communicator. When he was growing up, Erwin McManus was extremely reclusive, shy, and introverted. When he made public his call into vocational ministry, one of his relatives candidly commented, "We knew that God was calling your brother, but what is he going to do with you?" He didn't intend to be cruel; he simply was offering his assessment.

But God had big plans in mind for Erwin. His leadership and communication skills are incredible. Name a convention—he's probably spoken there. Name a country—he's probably spoken there. He leads a church of more than a thousand people in the heart of Los Angeles. They refer to themselves as a "nomadic church" since they meet in a variety of locations, though they're officially called Mosaic. Erwin's book *An Unstoppable Force* was a Gold Medallion finalist.

Erwin doesn't just turn on this style of communicating when he's in the pulpit. His preaching is merely an extension of his everyday life. Those who are close to him describe him as convicting, prophetic, and challenging. If you have listened to the segment on the audio CD, you already know that.

Interview With Erwin McManus

DAVE: When did you realize you were a great communicator?

ERWIN: I think I would rephrase the question. I came to Christ the week I turned twenty.

I had kind of a "God moment" in which God said to me, "If you will preach, I will meet you there." I always understood that my goal when I preached was to create an environment, a moment, where the presence of God was undeniable and a person was encountered by God. I never thought of myself as communicating; I felt that I was a portal. God promised that if I spoke his truth, he would meet me at an intersection where man would meet God and God would interact with man.

Through the years, of course, you hone skills, but at first there weren't any skills to hone! Yet people still were coming to Jesus Christ, and people's lives were being impacted.

DAVE: Tell me some different communicators who have influenced your style.

ERWIN: People who come to mind are those like Cecil B. DeMille and Steven Spielberg. Those are the two communicators I can point to before I was saved and after I was saved. I process things cinematically, not linearly, and so I think films have impacted me more than anything else. I have a "cinemagraphic" memory—I remember life in images and movements. I don't see life in snapshots and standstill. So that's also the way I communicate.

When I preach, I want to take you through an experience that you not only see but also feel as though you're a part of it. If I just translate a truth or transfer some information, I feel like I've wasted my time and yours. You know, you've been to a movie that's so great that you've forgotten you're in a theater; you've become a part of the experience. For me, that is what preaching is all about. It's literally about pulling people into an experience with God where they are translated into his presence and don't even know it's happened.

"When I preach, I want to take you through an experience that you not only see but also feel as though you're a part of it."

DAVE: How has your preaching style changed during twenty years of preaching?

ERWIN: My preaching has changed a lot.

DAVE: Were you more linear back then?

ERWIN: I tried to be linear, and I failed miserably. I tried the seminary thing where you take all the theological application from the commentaries, you get all the stories from all the historic books, and you just cut and paste your messages together. But that didn't work well. Now I don't try to be nonlinear or experiential—I just try to be me.

DAVE: What challenges must you overcome due to your natural style?

ERWIN: I don't really have any interest in preaching things I'm not passionate about. I don't really care about the "five steps to this" or "how to have a better that." I am essentially indifferent to helping you upgrade, so one of the dominant criticisms for me is that I hardly do any "how to's." I just got a message from John Maxwell, and he said I ask great questions but need to start giving answers. So one of my weaknesses is that I don't like giving any answers. I like asking enough questions to lead you to the same conclusion that I began with. I think it's more important to shape the framework from which people think and live than it is to fill the contents of that framework.

Another weakness is that what I say seems to appeal to people who are innovative and early adopters but has to be translated to the majority. That is something I have to deal with because, obviously, you want to preach to the masses. But my passion is in calling on those 3 percent or 4 percent of the culture who are the highest-octane leaders, thinkers, and innovators. Those people are the reason I get up every morning. That is what I live for, that is who I preach to. At times I really don't care if I effectively communicate to anyone else—and that is a weakness.

DAVE: Talk to me about your routine. Do you write out a manuscript?

ERWIN: No, I don't do a manuscript. Let me tell you a story. When my wife and I were first married, she said, "You need to prepare for your message; you're not preparing at all." She has a master's in theology, and she was watching me. I felt so guilty about the way I prepared to speak that I studied for two weeks for a message and wrote out notes. It was a catastrophe. The sermon was boring and disconnected. Afterward my wife said, "Don't ever prepare again." I think that from the outside looking in, it looks like I'm not prepared. But from the inside looking out, I know what I'm doing.

When I was right out of seminary, I was asked to speak in North Carolina. I had five pages of notes. We were in a prayer room before I preached, and I realized when I walked out on the stage, "Oh no! I don't have my notes." But then I thought, "You know what? Nothing in this world is going to stop me from communicating this message." I never used notes again. Right then God was saying to me, "Look, it's not about how you organize this thing; I'm just going to meet you right there." That really changed my life.

> "You know what? Nothing in this world is going to stop me from communicating this message."

Now I observe the world around me and try and see how the particular passage connects to reality. Then I try to flesh out that passage and see how my life would be different if I really believed it. I talk about Scripture being a portal that takes you into the presence of God.

DAVE: So your style of communicating is an outgrowth of what God is teaching you in your time in the Word.

ERWIN: If you know the Scriptures well enough, you can kind of surf through the Bible in your head. You have to have different tiers of information. First, what do the Scriptures say? Second, what does your life experience say about these Scriptures? Third, what human universals are true for everyone? I don't preach from the Scriptures to the person; I speak from the person to the Scriptures.

"In its essence, preaching translates us into the presence of God."

In its essence, preaching translates us into the presence of God. That is the only thing that gets me back up on Sunday. I really have no passion to just get up there and teach information.

DAVE: So your passion is for people to know Christ. You are wired to challenge people to know Christ.

ERWIN: Yeah, I'm passionate about returning this planet to the revolution Jesus Christ died for. That is what I think I'm wired for. I'll do whatever that takes, and communication is a big part of it.

You know that scene in *Braveheart* where all the troops are called to action? Every time I see that scene, I'm like, "Yeah! I want that!" I'm sitting there thinking, "Why can an actor invoke more enthusiasm about going to war and giving your life than a preacher who is calling people to advance the kingdom of God?" This is a fundamental dilemma with Christianity. I refuse to have the most breathtaking, inspiring, heart-pounding moments exist solely in the movies! To me, the tragedy of our time is that we are voyeurs who love feeling like we are part of something significant while we sit in our pews eating popcorn and drinking Diet Coke.

"To me, the tragedy of our time is that we are voyeurs who love feeling like we are part of something significant while we sit in our pews eating popcorn and drinking Diet Coke."

DAVE: Do you have any other specific goals when you preach or teach?

ERWIN: The goal of communication is creating a resonance. My prayer when I speak is, "God, I know you are speaking, so I don't want to override your voice. I want to resonate with it." So at first people hear me speaking. Then they stop hearing me and are having this conversation with God. That, to me, is really exciting. It changes everything. That is what makes speaking fun. Anything less is just teaching.

DAVE: You've mentioned before that when you speak at a Promise Keepers conference, you don't send a manuscript to them ahead of time.

ERWIN: I don't know what I'm going to talk about until I get there.

DAVE: Does it drive them crazy?

ERWIN: It does drive them crazy. I walk in, and I start getting a feel for the environment. But I do that everywhere, even at Mosaic. To me it is about the integrated experience. It is stepping into the moment that God is preparing and figuring out what it is that God is saying, doing, and exercising at that moment.

DAVE: You realize that your preparation and delivery mode is not typical. Many *try* to do that, but they end up rambling all over the place.

ERWIN: There is a difference between shooting from the hip and being able to improvise. When someone plays the piano without first learning the basic disciplines of piano, it's like a person who gets up to speak and rambles. But when someone has learned all the basics and can get up there and improvise and create melodies and sounds you've never heard before, that is another level. Both speakers might say, "I'm just freeflowin'." But freeflowin' that's disciplined is different from freeflowin' that has never been disciplined!

DAVE: What disciplines must you employ to make your communication style work?

ERWIN: Listening to God. That's the discipline. That's why I tell people, "You need to be in the Scriptures"—because you'll never know the voice of God unless you have the Scriptures just absolutely permeating your life.

Who would buy a $20,000 painting that was a paint-by-number? Who would pay someone just because he colored in the lines? We expect great artists to be able to *paint*, and great artists blend colors while they're painting. If you watch really high-level artists, they actually start painting layers of colors you never even see. They understand that there's a texture to their artistry that goes beyond surface-level vision.

I believe there's a similar difference in preaching. You've seen preachers who paint by numbers because that's how they were trained to do it. There wasn't a lot of freedom. They don't go with the flow when they sense something in the audience or a person. You ask me, "How can you remember your sermons?" The answer is that it's not something that is outside of me. It is who I am. That's why I could spend the next five days answering questions—because I'm not trying to remember information. It is integrated into the person I am.

"I try to make sure that my preaching is disturbing so it pulls people out of the moment and into eternity."

So when I'm preaching a sermon that *isn't* who I am, it's really tough. Then I really have to remember everything. I think preaching should be like telling your life story, like remembering something that happened. I experienced it. It is a part of who I am. It's not like I have to keep a detailed list of all the meaningful experiences of my life. I think that's the problem with asking, "Can other people do this?" Well, the real question is "Are they willing to pay the price to create a seamless relationship between themselves, the Scriptures, and God?" Preaching isn't about perfection. It isn't even about a level of refinement. If preaching is all about learning the structures and doctrines, then you better have a manuscript.

DAVE: What words would you use to describe your preaching?

ERWIN: Primal, dangerous, zealous, passionate. I want my preaching to be skewed. I try to make sure that my preaching is disturbing so it pulls people out of the moment and into eternity.

DAVE: What characteristics describe you?

ERWIN: I would prefer that people think of me as a warrior mystic or a mystic warrior. I don't want to leave out the mystical aspect of my life, my faith, and my preaching. That's probably more important to me than almost anything else.

A person can know he or she is a warrior mystic or a mystic warrior because they wake up every day with an acute sense of their own doubt and yet still enjoy life beyond reason. If there's a defining characteristic about how I live my life, it's this: I have a morbid sense of my own fatality. I can't escape it. Every day, I think about the fact that today could be the last day I live. And so I've translated that as "Today is a good day to die."

The guys who feel like they have their whole lives ahead are never going to lead a revolution. Right? They just have too much time on their hands. I would never hire anyone who golfs to my ministry team. They can like golfing—they just can't golf! I laugh and tell potential ministry staff that if they're joining this team, they aren't golfing again. You can play racquetball, basketball— anything that's fast—but if you like golf, you probably won't make it on this team. You want to suck the life out of this day because it could be your last one.

Every time I speak, I tell myself, "This may be the last message my kids ever hear." What do I want to say on this tape that I'm going to leave as a legacy to my children? What explanation am I going to give to them about why I was willing to risk everything and die and leave them fatherless? What is important enough to say for them to grow up the rest of their lives without me? If you don't communicate and think like that, I don't think you can lead a revolution.

Is it any surprise that Erwin has chosen as his life verse Jeremiah 20:9? The prophet Jeremiah says, "But if I say, 'I will not mention him or speak any more in his name,' his word is in my heart like a fire, a fire shut up in my bones. I am weary of holding it in; indeed, I cannot."

I have been fortunate to be friends with a couple of different CEOs of Fortune 500 companies. Both are extremely driven and focused individuals. Their tolerance for mediocrity is low, while their expectation of excellence is high. Erwin fits that mold perfectly. This personality carries over into his communication style because, as is often the case, his messages are an outpouring of his passion. He is consumed and conveys a sense of urgency.

I would have enjoyed digging into this more deeply with Erwin McManus, but I didn't want to be late for my tee time!

Advice on Refining This Style

◆ *Communicate the urgency of the moment.*

As you prepare a talk, think about appealing for responsive

action. Erwin is motivated by his children and keeps them at the forefront of his mind as he prepares. I loved his question "What do I want to say...that I'm going to leave as a legacy to my children?" Find something that lights a fire in *you* so you can light a fire in *others*. Remember: Your goal is to ignite a revolution!

Find something that lights a fire in *you* so you can light a fire in *others*.

◆ *Take a risk.*

Like blood to a shark, risk attracts Revolutionary Leaders. G. K. Chesterton said, "Courage is almost a contradiction in terms. It means a strong desire to live taking the form of a readiness to die."[4]

I'm reminded of when I'm playing golf and staring at a long second shot on a par 5. To reach the green will take a perfect shot of 220 yards—all carry, into a slight wind, and over a lake. Depending on my confidence level (and what I'm shooting for the round), I may not choose to risk landing in the water and adding a penalty stroke. But on other occasions, I'll grab my 3-wood and mannishly mutter, "I didn't come out here to lay up like some wimp." Then I swing, grunt, and pray. Usually the grunt adds an extra ten yards in pressure situations. If, per chance, the Lord should grin upon me and my ball should arrive safely on the green, I am elated. I get to enjoy every step of the next 220 yards as a reward for the risk I took.

You'll never lead a revolution if you repeatedly take the safest course of action. Too many communicators get set in their ways and grow content to just "lay up." But the sad reality is that, due to their conservatism, they will never have the chance to experience an eagle.

◆ *Use manuscripts for support.*

While you, too, can saturate yourself with God's Word and listen intently to God's voice, it takes an incredible gift to be able to stand before a congregation week after week without detailed preparation in written form. Erwin McManus is a uniquely gifted individual.

Writing a manuscript can bolster those who aren't as comfortable with this style and can act as a safeguard for those who don't normally use a manuscript. If you're going to go out on a limb and boldly tell it like it is, a word-for-word manuscript may protect you in the heat of the moment from saying something you didn't intend or may later regret. Your confidence will soar even though what you say will be daring.

Instead of always comforting the disturbed, try your hand at disturbing the comfortable.

◆ *Occasionally* **create** *problems.*
Erwin McManus says, "One of the most significant things a leader can do is not only identify problems and communicate them but actually *create* problems." This may not be the way most people think, but it's natural for Revolutionary Leaders. You can create problems by moving people out of their comfort zones. Instead of always comforting the disturbed, try your hand at disturbing the comfortable.

◆ ***Move your listeners out of their comfort zones with biblical truth.***
The most effective Revolutionary Leaders blend their intensity with a desire to be true to God's Word. John MacArthur wrote, "True biblical preaching ought to be a life-changing endeavor. The conscientious preacher does not merely seek to impart abstract doctrine or plain facts to his people; he also pleads with them for heartfelt and earnest obedience."[5]

Some Christian leaders shy away from sharing biblical passages because they don't want to scare people away. The Bible itself says Scripture is offensive, yet it becomes a magnet to those who are receptive. God's Word is filled with teachings that will revolutionize your life and the lives of your listeners.

◆ *Balance the menu for your congregation or class.*
Fight the tendency to avoid those topics with which you don't resonate. A full diet of revolutionary material can starve the believers of discipleship opportunities. Keep them well fed by being both daring and practical.

The challenge for the Revolutionary Leader is to maintain momentum during the mundane seasons of ministry. He or she must be able to consistently share the hope without all the hype. To do so requires planning what topics to teach and preach. Such planning allows those who embody this communication style to gear up during times when the speaking themes don't necessarily ignite their passion.

◆ Check your ego at the door.

Since this communication style wields such influence, be certain your marching orders are coming from God rather than your own agenda. Stay on the "narrow path" and point listeners to the Word and the Way.

◆ Don't forget how intimidating you can be.

While some people don't set out to intimidate others, it just kind of happens—the same way middle-aged men collect lint in their bellybuttons by the end of each day. There is no scientific explanation for either phenomenon. They just happen. Revolutionary Leaders may be perceived as so intense that their single-minded focus becomes a double-edged sword. It can either frighten or inspire the listener—and sometimes both!

> While some people don't set out to intimidate others, it just kind of happens—the same way middle-aged men collect lint in their bellybuttons by the end of each day.

Erwin's very language shows that he is on the offensive and is aggressive for Christ. Admittedly, some personality types will bristle at the high-power word choices. But Erwin's revolutionary methods are shared in a *radical* way, not an *obnoxious* way. While I see this as a strength, it also must be a caution.

To avoid intimidating your listeners, you can intentionally slow down your speaking rate. Calm yourself as you speak. If you stay in fifth gear all the time, you run the risk of wearying your listeners so much that they tune you out.

◆ Remain strong in the face of intimidation.

Patricia Heaton, a Christian, plays the role of Raymond's wife in the hit sitcom *Everybody Loves Raymond*. She is outspoken and coura-geous in her beliefs, walking out of the American Music Awards and speaking out against abortion. Heaton says, "When my final judg-ment comes, I don't think I'll be answering to Barbra Streisand."[6] I suspect that Patricia Heaton is a Revolutionary Leader.

If you lead a Bible study or teach a class, don't be held hostage by the critical spirit of a few. Teaching, preaching, and serving invite the scrutiny of followers. Stay the course, and lead a spiri-tual upheaval. Remember these words from Jesus: "Do not be afraid of those who kill the body but cannot kill the soul. Rather, be afraid of the One who can destroy both soul and body in hell" (Matthew 10:28). Jude 1:23a says, "Snatch others from the fire and save them."

ENDNOTES

1 Joel Barker, *LeaderSHIFT: Five Lessons for Leaders in the 21st Century* (training video).

2 Tony Campolo, comments (Louisville, KY: North American Christian Convention, July 1981).

3 Campolo, comments, North American Christian Convention.

4 Gilbert K. Chesterton, *Orthodoxy* (New York, NY: Stratford Press, Inc., 1908), 170.

5 Michael Fabarez, *Preaching That Changes Lives*, Foreword by John MacArthur (Nashville, TN: Thomas Nelson, Inc., 2002), i. Used by permission of Thomas Nelson, Inc.

6 Terry Mattingly, "Ministry and Media: Irony Abounds—Year 15," The Lookout (May 25, 2003), 14.

CHAPTER 5

The Engaging Humorist

"Jokes are not the best way to be humorous, but the ability to laugh at oneself, at the world around you, or at the human condition can really open your audience to like you. Remember that comedy is not your goal, but *connection* is."
—**H e r s h a e l   Y o r k** [1]

"A cheerful heart is good medicine, but a crushed spirit dries up the bones." —**P r o v e r b s   1 7 : 2 2**

The Engaging Humorist speaks to help people *enjoy* something.
The target is the listener's *funny bone*.
Think Ken Davis.

Similar styles: Persuasive Motivator, Relevant Illustrator, Unorthodox Artist

Words that describe this style: Funny, compelling, affable, entertaining, winsome, humorous, creative

You might be an Engaging Humorist if...
- you often "milk" a laugh but rarely step on a laugh.
- your teachers early on in life told your parents that you had the gift of gab.
- once you hear a joke, you can tell it in detail—and can even improve it.
- an ad-lib you stumble upon during your sermon goes over so well that you spend the rest of the message fearful that you'll forget it before you can write it down.
- memorizing a joke, setting it up, and delivering the punch

line come very naturally for you.

- you include a joke early on in your talk to relax yourself more than your audience.
- you prefer the adrenaline rush of taking a stab at high-risk humor over delivering typical, low-risk humor anyone can attempt.

About This Style

A number of years ago, I went to visit a church member in a local hospital. I confidently strode to the nurses' station and asked which room the patient was in. I'd been in the room for about a minute when a young nurse with a clipboard entered and dutifully stood beside me. I noticed that after every question I asked, she was recording the patient's answer. Eventually I mentioned our church to the man. Embarrassed, the nurse stopped writing, looked at me, and slowly asked, "You're not the doctor?"

I said, "No, I preach. I don't practice!"

I used this story to begin a message on living a consistently Christian life. Everyone can relate to incorrectly sizing up a situation as the nurse did. The humor relaxed the congregation and allowed me to frame the rest of my talk. I continued by saying that while I was proud of my quick reply, I've come to realize it's sometimes a true description of me. I preach. I don't always practice what I preach. And hypocrisy is never a laughing matter. Jesus says in Matthew 5:20 that our righteousness must surpass that of the religious leaders. In other words, he prefers that I practice instead of just preach.

Love and laughter can break down the strongest of defenses, softening a hardened heart and relaxing a tense individual.

A sense of humor is *so* important in communicating. It can have such a positive impact on how the audience receives your serious points. Love and laughter can break down the strongest of defenses, softening a hardened heart and relaxing a tense individual. Even mild comedy can win a listener's attention, allowing you to engage the listener on a new level.

Some—John Wesley, for example—have had the idea that there is no place for humor in the pulpit. In contrast, G.

Campbell Morgan thought preaching was the highest form of fun available. There is laughter and life in growing churches, and that's part of the reason people want to be there. Appropriate humor, strategically placed, can be like a breath of fresh air to a person who's been underwater for a minute. Humor also gives the audience permission to audibly respond—preferably with laughter! Dryness is a goal for underarms, not speakers!

As you read other chapters in this book, you may be surprised to discover that you fit a certain style. That will *not* be the case with this chapter. Engaging Humorists most likely have known their stripes for quite some time. She may have been the class clown. He probably enjoyed the limelight at a very young age. These communicators may have grown up using humor as a defense mechanism. Perhaps it allowed them to lighten tense moments or avoid confrontation with some bully. And now, years later, they are able to hone this gift through their speaking, writing, or preaching.

The Engaging Humorist tends to rely on natural talent rather than painstaking preparation. The reason is simple: This man or woman prefers the crowd to the discipline of sitting in an empty room with commentaries and a computer keyboard. Maybe that explains why so many Engaging Humorists end up in ministry. Ministry provides a built-in opportunity to "perform" in front of a crowd.

The Engaging Humorist is one of the communication styles I naturally relate to. When I was in the ninth grade, my father got a record album by a Christian speaker named Don Lonie. He was on the cutting edge of Christian comedy in the 1960s. Knowing my reputation as a class clown, Dad informed me that this man used humor to share the gospel. Early on, I saw how laughter could build a bridge to Christ. When choosing a career, I wrestled between comedy and ministry. Those are not the strange bedfellows they first appear to be. Both vocations require communicating in such a way that people are motivated to respond in some way. A secular comedian desires laughter; a preacher, life change.

Simple logic indicates that Jesus had a great sense of humor. He captivated crowds for hours. Children flocked to him. Think about it: He's the ultimate friend. People of all temperaments say they look for a sense of humor in a friend. The ability to laugh at yourself and with others is paramount in building relationships, and Jesus related to people of all backgrounds.

If you aren't naturally wired in this art, this chapter will help you to grow in your use of humor. You can use humor to engage your audience in active listening. You can use it to set up a conclusion to a heavy or lengthy segment. Humor provides a break and can relax listeners before you move in and allow the Word of God to pierce their hearts.

Jesus, an Engaging Humorist

Jesus must have had a great sense of humor. On several occasions, an angry church member has shaken a Bible in my face and said, "You show me one joke in this book." I usually begin by taking the person to the Sermon on the Mount. This discourse is laced with humor. Back when Christ was preaching, the humor of Jewish culture was based on hyperbole. Any gross exaggeration would elicit a belly laugh. That's why Jesus spoke with vivid word pictures that, through laughter, drove home the point while softening his listeners' hearts. So when Christ said, "Why do you look at the speck of sawdust in your brother's eye and pay no attention to the plank in your own eye?" (Matthew 7:3) people weren't reverently responding, "Amen." Instead, they were probably laughing. In the midst of the laughter, his point was made. Later Jesus said, "Again I tell you, it is easier for a camel to go through the eye of a needle than for a rich man to enter the kingdom of God" (Matthew 19:24). Jesus knew that humor was a great equalizer. Perhaps that's why he created it.

Simple logic indicates that Jesus had a great sense of humor.

A college professor once described the church where I serve in one word. She chose the word *joy*. What a compliment! Jesus said he came so that we could have life more abundantly. The New International Version reads, "Have [life] to the full" (John 10:10). I firmly believe Christians should be the happiest people on the face of the earth. They can enjoy this life because they know where they will spend the next—for all eternity.

Ken Davis, an Engaging Humorist

You are in for a treat. Ken Davis is a Christian comedian who has a list of kudos as long as Shaquille O'Neal's arm. In a regular week, he may speak for a church, entertain a secular company or business organization, and perform comedy for ten to twenty thousand at the National Quartet Convention or Praise Gathering.

Ken's Dynamic Communicators Workshops fill up quickly because he's more than a comedian. He's a gifted speaker who knows more about the art of humor than anyone I know. But he also teaches people how to be more effective communicators.

Interview With Ken Davis

DAVE: When did you first realize you had the gift of communication?

KEN: I was a sophomore or junior in high school, and I had a wonderful English teacher, Frances W. Peterson. One day she made me stay after class because I'd gotten into trouble for using some crude humor. I thought she was going to expel me, but her first words to me were "God has given you a gift."

I was not expecting those words. Mrs. Peterson went on to say, "Now you're using this gift to destroy my class, and that is going to change. I want you to go out for speech."

I said, "I'm not going out for speech. All my friends go around school with macho symbols on their jackets—hockey sticks, footballs. I'm not going to walk around school with a set of lips on my jacket!"

She laughed and said, "Yes, you will, because you won't like the alternative."

So basically, she made me do it. I went on to win every contest I ever entered. Mrs. Peterson was willing to dig through the dirt and see the gold. She was the first to say, "God has given you a gift."

DAVE: Which communicators have influenced your style?

KEN: Bill Cosby. Haddon Robinson. I like to listen to Chuck Colson and Tony Campolo, but I don't use their style. I love to listen to my own pastor at People's Church in Franklin, Tennessee—Rick White.

Bill Cosby has had more of an effect on me than I realized. He's a comedian who doesn't tell jokes. He tells stories. I just admire his style. I also liked the Smothers Brothers; their humor also was more observational.

"You can be as good as me. I guarantee it. Prepare a message tomorrow, then deliver it one hundred times over five years."

You know what I do? Sometimes I tell jokes that you'll never recognize. I take the joke and turn it into a story. Bill Cosby told exaggerated stories. Were all of them true? Not on your life. But they came out of real-life experiences.

DAVE: What's the biggest challenge for you to overcome due to your natural style?

KEN: Let me just admit that I'm still overcoming challenges. One is that my style and ability allow me to step onstage unprepared and still do well. That is not good. Another challenge is that I have so much material to wing it with and a new audience every time, so I can get away with *not* developing new material. But that's not good. The challenge is to continue to seek freshness, even as I deliver messages I've done before—to continue to research and refine to make them better.

In our seminars I tell people, "You can be as good as me. I guarantee it. Prepare a message tomorrow, then deliver it one hundred times over five years. Of course you can be good."

But then I'm quick to point out that I admire the pastor who gets up week after week and delivers a powerful, engaging, focused, and crystal-clear message. He has to write new stories, new jokes, new ideas with a new focus every week. That's the essence of a great communicator.

DAVE: Do you manuscript?

KEN: No, that's another one of my weaknesses. I should. If I did manuscript and tried to read it, it would ruin my style. But I believe that manuscripting is extremely powerful because it allows you to become a wordsmith. If I disciplined myself to manuscript, to spend more time writing and rewriting jokes, I'd become a more powerful communicator and a more powerful comedian. My personal opinion is that you shouldn't read verbatim from a manuscript in the pulpit. But I do think you should go through the work of preparing one. It will make your message much better.

DAVE: Do you ever ad-lib and it goes over so well that through the rest of the talk you're wondering if you'll be able to remember it?

KEN: Sure. And then when the talk is done, all I can remember is that something good happened. One time as I came off the stage, I grabbed a guy who had heard me numerous times and said to him, "Somewhere in my talk, I said something brand new. You're not leaving the room until you tell me what it was!" I think he's still standing in that room!

DAVE: Tell us some disciplines that help make your communication more effective.

KEN: I'm always taking notes. I take notes as I watch the news or read a magazine or listen to someone speaking. Then my mind uses what's happening as a springboard for ideas. This even happens with my own talks. The other night I was talking about Hebrews 12:1-2—running the race with perseverance. And I got this idea to say, "You know what? A lot of people will try to convince you that you're going to win the race. But God doesn't care who wins the race. In reality, we're all running in the Special Olympics—all of us are challenged in some way. If we finish, we win."

DAVE: How can preachers and teachers make their audiences want to listen to them?

KEN: The challenge is to make the audience know that they can relate to you. In the midst of what we say, there has to be integrity and honesty and vulnerability. That's why I love humor. Someone said, "Humor is a gentle way to acknowledge human frailty; vulnerability is built into it."

Nothing harms relationships with others or God more than trying to perpetuate the perception of perfection. It's hogwash.

We're not pointing people to ourselves; we're pointing people to Christ. Humor is a gentle way to bring people, no matter what they've done, to the foot of the Cross. Humor lets them know that there is grace and forgiveness. I'm reaching for the person in the back row who doesn't think he even deserves to be in the same building because the name Jesus is being mentioned there. That's the guy I'm reaching for because I've been there.

"Humor is a gentle way to bring people, no matter what they've done, to the foot of the Cross."

DAVE: Let's talk about facial expressions and voice changes.

KEN: Voice changes are like walking a tight rope. You don't want to create a different character with every sentence or it becomes corny. But sometimes you create a character with your voice and actions to undo a false impression people have of a Bible character. People see Moses as a Charlton Heston, but Moses tried everything in his power to get out of following God's call. So I developed this shaky voice to convey the doubt and fear Moses was experiencing.

Listening to myself on tape has been the greatest help in working on my voice. It has helped me overcome some very annoying habits. I learned that I had a way of laughing at my own stories that was just extremely annoying, so I stopped doing it. I also recognized a high register in my voice—a nasal, whiny sound that I've almost totally eliminated. But listening also helps you recognize some things that are effective.

Reviewing video of your talks is excellent for critiquing things like facial expressions. When it comes to expressions, the more subtle they are, the better. Just raise an eyebrow. Something that subtle will be seen. You *could* make a big facial expression, but it may be better to just look at the audience. Johnny Carson was a master at this. Look at audience, look at desk, then look up.

DAVE: Some will read this chapter and say, "This style is me." Others will not. How do you take people who feel that they're a "four" in the humor department up to a "six" or "seven"?

KEN: Know what makes something funny. There are volumes written on this, but basically it comes down to three things. One:

exaggeration. Repeating something God said may not be funny, but saying it in a deep voice may be. Two: truth. Helping people see simple truths that they ordinarily overlook can be hilarious. Three: surprise. Surprise is joke humor. People who don't think they're humorous probably shouldn't try a bunch of surprise.

DAVE: Give me an example, if you don't mind.

KEN: Let me give you an example of truth being used as humor. On the way to church, the kids are fighting in the back seat over stuff that makes no sense whatsoever. I look at the audience and ask, "Have you ever heard this coming from the back seat: 'Dad, she's looking at me!'" There's nothing exaggerative about that, no element of surprise. It's simple truth. Yet it never fails to get a laugh. High risk can bring high reward.

There are two kinds of humor: high-risk and low-risk. In high-risk, you start a joke by saying, "You're going to love this." It's already high-risk humor because you've set up an expectation. You've said, "Stand on the rug. I'm going to jerk it out from under you, and you're going to love it."

Here's another example of high-risk humor: "Two parrots walked into a bar..." It's high-risk humor because the audience immediately recognizes that you're telling a joke.

Here's an example of low-risk humor that really happened in our home:

I walk into the house. My daughter has a twenty-pound fishing line tied to her tooth. She's probably five. She has the other end tied to a doorknob. She's slamming the door, her little head is jerking, spit is flying out of her mouth.

I ask, "What are you doing?"

She says, "I'm pulling my tooth."

I go over, feel the tooth, and say, "It's not loose."

She looks up at me and says, "Leave me alone. I need money!"

If you want to learn to be humorous, recognize the humor in a story. This one made me laugh, so I tell the story.

The point I drive home with the story is that you've got to read between the lines. You've got to realize that sometimes what your children are saying to you isn't really what they need or want. My daughter isn't trying to pull her tooth; she's trying to get five bucks. If people don't laugh, that's OK. Do it again another time, and try to figure out a way to strengthen it a little bit.

Know your own style and ability. I'm the kind of guy who wants to see people rolling on the floor, clutching their sides, with stuff shooting out their noses. Not everybody is that kind of humorist. Today we think of humorists as stand-up comedians. That is one tiny sliver. Mark Twain is known as one of the greatest humorists who ever lived. He had the ability to shove in the knife and turn it so you say, "Whoa, that is so true." People like Twain or Will Rogers were humorists, not comedians. Garrison Keillor is a much more contemporary example. That guy doesn't put people on the floor. He makes them chuckle and remember things they forgot long, long ago. So if you're at a party and you're the person who tells a story that makes people say, "Oh, that's so true," then that's the kind of humorist you are. Don't try to be the stand-up comedian. You don't need to be like Ken Davis or Bill Cosby in order to use humor.

> "Ecclesiastes says there's 'a time to laugh.' Humor is a gift from God."

DAVE: How do you handle the people who criticize the use of humor and say there is no place for humor when Christian leaders speak?

KEN: I'd like to tell them to lighten up and get a life. Certainly there's a place for humor. Ecclesiastes says there's "a time to laugh." Humor is a gift from God. It shouldn't be left out.

A lady once said to me, "The gospel doesn't need all the frivolity you bring to it!"

I tried to be kind, but I said, "Is that so? Where do you go to church?"

She proudly told me. I asked, "Do you have missionaries?"

"Of course," she replied.

I went on, "Do you send your missionaries to foreign countries?" She replied, "Yes."

Then I asked, "Do you just send them over, or do they get some kind of training?"

"No," she answered. "They go for a year or so of training."

I continued, "What do they train the missionaries to do?"

"To present the gospel in the context of the culture they're going into," she said.

I said, "Ma'am, if you believe in Jesus Christ and you live in the United States of America, you are living in a foreign culture. You're just passing through this culture. And this culture won't even stop to listen to your gospel unless it's presented in a context they'll listen to. We live in a culture saturated with humor and entertainment. Maybe in another century and at another time, humor didn't have much of a place. But in this culture and at this time, God is using it greatly."

During our conversation, Ken Davis mentioned that his passion in communication is evangelism. In other words, there's a goal behind his humor. There's a method to the madness. He says, "You have to have a singular focus when you start. I know what my focus is, and everything in the message comes back to that focus."

Advice on Refining This Style

◆ *Get to know* me!

Humor is a combination of body language, facial expressions, eye contact, voice inflection, rate of delivery, timing, and—of course—the words you use. In my book, familiarity can breed humor. The better your class or church knows you, the funnier a facial expression or phrase becomes.

Over time as you share your own vulnerability, personal joys, and defeats, these enhance the possibilities for humor. When your audience better understands you, they better understand the humor in a situation. They may even get ahead of you. If you listen to Ken Davis on the accompanying CD, you'll sometimes hear premature laughter from audience members who have previously heard him expound on similar topics.

◆ *Self-deprecation pays big dividends.*

Show some vulnerability by telling more stories in which you're the joke rather than the hero. Some teachers and preachers enjoy putting themselves on a spiritual pedestal for all to gaze upon, but they'll never measure up to their listeners' expectations. In addition, the flock won't feel comfortable going to their shepherd if they don't think you're able to relate to their struggles.

Humor shows humanness. Some of my favorite speakers are those who occasionally sprinkle a dose of self-deprecating humor into the mix. Don't miss the power of such an intentional inclusion, which makes the communicator more authentic and approachable.

The personal story about the flat tire on your family vacation is almost always better than the anecdote in the joke book.

◆ *Tickle their funny bones with reality humor.*
The best humorists make observations about real-life experiences. The personal story about the flat tire on your family vacation is almost always better than the anecdote in the joke book.

If something you experienced seems funny, bounce it off other people. If they don't smile or a laugh, keep looking. But if they do, file the story for future use. Real-life stories deliver humor throughout instead of just at the punch line. (Listen to my audio clip on the CD.) And your listeners can relate better to reality humor, which makes meaningful application more natural.

◆ *Write down material that lends itself to humor.*
Ken Davis said he's always taking notes as he reads, watches, and listens. You hear the same jokes and stories he does. Take your humor to the next level by writing down what you hear and keeping it so you can retrieve it. My philosophy is if something made me laugh, it can make others laugh too. Don't worry about *how* you'll use it—just get it into your computer or on paper. Someday there may be a perfect fit.

◆ *Stay within the realm of your natural style—low-risk or high-risk humor.*
Take to heart Ken's explanation and encouragement on whether to use high-risk humor or low-risk humor. In my opinion, there

are few things more grating than watching a person who isn't funny try to be funny. But everyone—whether the high-risk storyteller or the dry-witted, introverted intellectual—has some style of humor that can work.

If your typical preference is not to use much humor, then don't try to catapult yourself into the world of high-risk humor. Stretching can be good for you, but a wholesale overnight change confuses your congregation.

◆ Beware of using humor as an arrow.

You may be tempted to pick on the same staff people or church members, but too much humor directed at the same target can backfire. A fine line also exists between humor and sarcastically belittling someone. Don't overdo it. If your humor predictably targets the same people or carries even a hint of malice, the audience will feel awkward or sorry for those individuals. Remember, the goal of humor is to relax your listeners, not to make them tense.

◆ Use humorous illustrations when they naturally fit.

I thoroughly enjoy crafting a humorous, real-life story and then making the transition into the spiritual application. Last year my sister-in-law Amy called and told me that her daughter's pet bunny had been put to sleep. The vet's office was going to close at 6 p.m., Amy was running late, and she needed me to pick up the dead bunny from the vet. The dead bunny's name was "Happy." Well, the juxtaposition of the deceased's name and my conversation with the vet staff provided me with plenty of humorous fodder.

> There are few things more grating than watching a person who isn't funny try to be funny.

This happened on a Thursday, and the story amazingly found its way into my message that weekend! It provoked numerous bursts of laughter and provided a pretty decent application. I even was able to weave the story into my conclusion to drive home a serious point.

Honestly, I felt quite proud of the way I'd worked in the story and of the response I'd gotten. The story had registered an "eight" on a scale from one to ten. I savored the taste for a few weeks until my annual evaluation meeting, when Bob Russell (my senior minister) and I discussed preaching. Bob challenged me to wait for the perfect fit instead of forcing it. Though he acknowledged that I'd come a long way in this area, he said that continuing to fine-tune would improve my preaching. He brought up the "Happy" story. He said, "You made it fit, but it wasn't a natural outgrowth of your text or topic. It was a good fit but not a great fit."

Then he said the words that crushed this Engaging Humorist: "What if you had saved the 'Happy' story for your sermon about the Resurrection this coming Easter?"

Ouch. At that moment, speaking the truth in love had lost its luster to this recipient of the truth. You have to understand the situation. This was *the* year. For the first time, Bob was allowing me to fly solo on Easter with about twenty-eight thousand passengers on board.

But he was right. I had succumbed to temptation, had eaten the fruit of the "easy way out," and had been thoroughly satisfied with my "eight" on the laugh-o-meter. Later that year when I began to work on my Easter message, I opened my "stories" file to find it empty. I felt like a sixteen-year-old who'd gotten the car keys from his father only to find the gas tank on E.

Here's the takeaway: If you find yourself working into your message what's happened since your last message, you're probably forcing some stories. Keep digging and working. Don't settle for the immediate "eight" when you could wait for the perfect placement that makes a story become a "nine" or even a "ten." Ask a trusted friend or ministry partner to tell you honestly if your planned attempt at humor fits or is forced. When it comes to humor, patience always beats impulsiveness.

◆ *Balance humor throughout the whole message or lesson.*
Television shows take watchers through all sorts of ups and downs. Their goal is to tie everything together and end on an upbeat note. The same often is true for sermons. But too much humor—or not enough—will cause your listeners to tune you out. One way to protect against this is to color-code your lessons

or sermons. I go through my manuscript with some high-lighters—Scriptures in blue, outline points in green, humor in pink, quotes in purple, and key words in stories in orange. Then by just glancing at a layout, I can tell if the sermon ebbs and flows well. If I'm overloading or lacking humor—or any other ele-ment—I can quickly address the imbalance.

◆ *Think* quality *humor, not* quantity.

J. Michael Shannon, a preaching professor at Cincinnati Bible College and Seminary, compares a danger in preaching to his mother's early attempts to feed him broccoli. He refused to eat broccoli as a child, so she tried to trick him into eating it. She called it "little trees" and encour-aged him to eat the leaves off the trees. It didn't work. Finally, she discovered that he'd eat broccoli if she put cheese on it.

> Humor can be a great asset when used sparingly—as a sidelight, not the spotlight.

"I don't think there's anything wrong with entertain-ment value in our sermons," Shannon says. "There's nothing wrong with putting a little cheese on our broccoli. The problem comes if we feed people nothing *but* cheese. It's impor-tant for us not to forget the broccoli."[2]

If you tend to win over your listeners by entertaining them, you may condition them to ignore everything but your jokes. Fight the temptation of working in the best joke you've heard since your last sermon or lesson. Humor can be a great asset when used sparingly—as a sidelight, not the spotlight.

◆ *Wordsmith your material.*

Before telling a humorous story or joke, go over the precise word-ing with a fine-toothed comb. Continue to make tiny adjustments so the story can elicit the best response. For example, I've heard people say, "I'd like to be humble, but what if no one notices?" It's a great line that's funnier when written than when spoken because it comes so quickly that many people miss the joke. But if I add one word, that risk is reduced. So I say, "I've heard peo-ple *facetiously* say, 'I'd like to be humble, but what if no one notices?'" My addition tips off the congregation to expect something humorous, and they respond accordingly.

◆ *Practice telling jokes or humorous stories so that the punch line flows.*
Sometimes I'll hear Bob Russell tell a story three times before he uses it in a weekend message. Try out your humor during all your lunch appointments throughout the week or in a staff meeting. You'll likely make minor adjustments that will increase your comfort when sharing it in your message or lesson.

◆ *Use technology to your advantage.*
Several months ago, I was preaching about how we shouldn't allow Satan to get a foothold in our lives through addictive habits. Finally I said, "Do you know what we need to do? As a great theologian once said…"

At that moment, the congregation broke into laughter and applause. I didn't even finish the phrase. Why? Because as soon as I gave the cue—"as a great theologian once said"—the video tech crew popped this up on the screen: " 'Nip it in the bud.'—Barney Fife, theologian."

If you expend the extra effort, one line amazingly can give people some comic relief. Then you've got them right back with you, and they're primed to listen.

◆ *Create an exit strategy for failed attempts at humor.*
No true Engaging Humorist attempts high-risk humor without a plan B. Should the joke end, only to be met with silence or groans, have a strategy for emerging from the fallout caused by the "bomb." If I try a joke in the first of multiple services and it bombs, I'll sometimes reach into my pocket, pull out a pen, dramatically mark out a portion of my manuscript, and say, "Won't use that one next hour." Or, with a straight face, I might use the old line "I thought that joke was pretty funny. I seem to be alone in that assessment."

Humor also comes in handy with distractions. Sometimes

when microphones squeal, I'll pause and say, "That concludes the musical portion of our program."

To respond to that once-a-year, bloodcurdling, ear-piercing sound surge that can throw you and the audience totally off, pause for three seconds before saying, "We're going to try to continue if you'll just give me a minute to go change my pants!" The congregation went crazy with laughter when I said that. It borders on crude, but no one will be offended by your honest reaction to an extremely piercing sound!

Once when a cell phone rang during the middle of the service—it will happen to you—a preacher said, "Don't take that call unless it's Jesus. If it's Jesus, we want to talk to him."

People may respond to these lines with affirmations such as "You're so spontaneous!" But the truth is that you merely had an exit strategy. I call this "rehearsed spontaneity"—waiting for a particular situation to arise, then instantly pulling the most effective line from your memory bank.

ENDNOTES

1 Hershael York, "Making the Point with SHARP Illustrations," Preaching magazine (July-August, 2003), 19.

2 J. Michael Shannon, comments (Indianapolis, IN: Preaching Summit, March 24, 2003).

CHAPTER **6**

The Convincing Apologist

"God doesn't ask us to take a blind leap of faith into the darkness, but he does ask us to take a step of faith into the light."
—**Norm Geisler**[1]

"But in your hearts set apart Christ as Lord. Always be prepared to give an answer to everyone who asks you to give the reason for the hope that you have. But do this with gentleness and respect, keeping a clear conscience, so that those who speak maliciously against your good behavior in Christ may be ashamed of their slander."
—**1 Peter 3:15-16**

The Convincing Apologist speaks to help people *believe* something. The target is the listener's *worldview*. Think Lee Strobel.

Similar styles: Persuasive Motivator, Scholarly Analytic, Cultural Prophet, Passionate Teacher

Words that describe this style: Logical, pragmatic, systematic, certain, influential, defender, supporter, protector, champion

You might be a Convincing Apologist if...

- substantiating your sources is a high priority in building credibility.
- you have always had an interest in apologetics.
- you take on the role of prosecuting attorney or defense attorney in arguments with others.
- you're willing to "crockpot" spiritual growth rather than "microwave" it.

- you prefer *Law & Order* to *Friends* reruns.
- your IQ is above average—or at least is higher than that of this book's author.
- you love to defend the Bible—especially to skeptics.

About This Style

Some laborers were laying a drain across a college campus when they uncovered a power cable directly in their path. They suspected that it was only an abandoned line, but they called the campus electrical department and asked for someone to identify it just to be safe. An electrician arrived, looked at the cable, and assured the laborers it was a dead line.

"Just cut it out of your way," the electrician said.

One of the crew asked, "Are you sure there's no danger?"

The electrician replied, "I'm sure."

The workman said, "Well, then, can you cut it for us?"

The electrician hesitated a moment and then, with a slight smile, said, "I'm not *that* sure."

Some people demand more evidence than others—especially regarding eternal matters. Like electrical wires, issues of faith are too important to approach with a casual or cavalier attitude. Each listener individually must decide whether to accept or reject Christianity. Some want every "i" dotted and every "t" crossed before they make a commitment to Christ. It is specifically for those individuals that God created a group of communicators we call the Convincing Apologists.

I know I'm not supposed to envy, but I do envy those adept at this communication style. The heartbeat of the Convincing Apologist is to systematically communicate so as to sway the listener to embrace the rational truth of Scripture. These communicators make no outlandish appeals, no emotional requests. They bypass the heart and go after the head with logical, substantiated arguments. Read a book by a Convincing Apologist, and the footnotes will wear you out. Validation and verification become second nature as these communicators slowly chip away at the defensive barriers nonbelievers raise. One by one, with help from

God's Spirit and Word, the walls slowly come down.

Ravi Zacharias said, "A man rejects God neither because of intellectual demands nor because of the scarcity of evidence. A man rejects God because of a moral resistance that refuses to admit his need for God."[2] We will not hear God's voice or see God's face or be eyewitnesses of the Resurrection in this life. However, accepting Christ is not committing intellectual suicide. Plenty of evidence supports what we believe. We simply must come to the end of all we can read and study and reason and experience…and take one more step—the step of faith.

Some of the more emotional communication styles—the Inspiring Orator, the Revolutionary Leader, the Persuasive Motivator—may more quickly evoke a decision from listeners. Those of you who fall into the category of Convincing Apologist, though, have been gifted by God to make disciples that last. One reason Convincing Apologists are effective over the long haul is that they look at all sides of an issue. Each proof they articulate adds to building an airtight case that can't be punctured.

> Stephen Brown honestly admits, "If you have never had a question about your faith, you probably don't have much of a faith."

Those who are more cerebral and who come to faith through study often become Convincing Apologists. Lee Strobel, Josh McDowell, Lew Wallace (author of *Ben-Hur*), and C.S. Lewis come to mind. Each overcame doubt through his personal search, along with the influence of those with this communication style.

Plenty more people still need to be convinced of the gospel message. Some have never made a decision; others have but endure a shaky faith. Stephen Brown honestly admits, "If you have never had a question about your faith, you probably don't have much of a faith."[3]

Matt Proctor observed that Convincing Apologists address listeners' worldview. Your worldview is the defining system or code of authority in your life. It directs your decision-making. Some people's worldview is driven by popular opinion; others look out for number one. But God's Word drives the Christian's worldview. Convincing Apologists try to *reshape* the worldview of non-Christians and *buttress* the worldview of Christians.

Newsweek magazine carried an article about Carl Sagan titled "Unbeliever's Quest." It conveyed that the author and astronomer wanted proof, not prayers. Apparently, despite the many people who tried to convince Sagan of God's existence, he refused to concede. Even as his bout with cancer drew his life to a close, he maintained his doubt. His wife said, "There was no deathbed conversion, no appeals to God, no hope for an afterlife, no pretending that he and I, who had been inseparable for 20 years, were not saying goodbye forever."

Convincing Apologists try to *reshape* the worldview of non-Christians and *buttress* the worldview of Christians.

She was asked, "Didn't Carl want to believe?"

She replied fiercely, "Carl never wanted to believe. He wanted to *know*."[4]

The tragedy is that he knows now, and it's too late. I'm convinced that there aren't many Carl Sagans reading this book, but there are plenty of people sitting in your classrooms and sanctuaries who have questions and uncertainties about Christianity.

Together, let's see if you're a Convincing Apologist. If you aren't, let's see what you can learn from those who are. Who knows? You may find you have the ability to convince your listeners to embrace a biblical worldview.

Jesus, a Convincing Apologist

When Jesus communicated, he wanted his audience to believe. Just as a Convincing Apologist would, he targeted changing his listeners' worldview. Jesus would remind his listeners about life within their current worldview; then he would offer a contrast with his suggested course of action. For example, Jesus says in Matthew 5:38-39, "You have heard that it was said, 'Eye for eye, and tooth for tooth.' But I tell you, Do not resist an evil person. If someone strikes you on the right cheek, turn to him the other also."

Later, in verse 44, Jesus radically challenges the crowd to love their enemies. He points out that all people love their friends—big deal! Someone with a different worldview would try this distinctive approach!

There is only one reason to follow Jesus' suggestions: Your

worldview is focused on living for eternity rather than for the here and now. The motivation for loving enemies and turning the other cheek is to gain the right to be heard and so to lead your enemies to eternal salvation.

Lee Strobel, a Convincing Apologist

Our featured Convincing Apologist emerged from doubt and confusion with a firm faith that is grounded in truth, maybe because he wrestled with it more than most of us.

Lee Strobel didn't start out seeking, though. He was an atheist who was a top journalist in Chicago. He went with his wife to a church service in order to poke holes in what was taking place there. Instead, his worldview was challenged. He began an intensive search to see if there was a God who could be known and worshipped. Eventually, he gave his life to Christ. He joined the teaching team at Willow Creek Community Church, and a few years later he joined the teaching team at Saddleback Community Church. With the incredible success of his books, he presently spends the majority of his time writing and trying to influence evangelism in any way he can.

Interview With Lee Strobel

DAVE: When did you sense that you had a gift for communication?

LEE: I came to Christ in 1981 and entered the ministry in 1987. By that time, I was thirty-five years old or something. It's funny… I felt like God had given me a gift in terms of communicating, speaking, and preaching, but I also felt that there was so much danger of self-interest, self-promotion, self-aggrandizement. So I prayed about it. I thought, "Maybe this is just me. Maybe I don't have a gift. So I'm not going to do anything about this gift until somebody tells me they see it in me and encourages me to develop it." So I just gave it to God.

About two years after I came to service ministries at Willow Creek, Bill Hybels said to me, "The elders have been talking, and we really believe that God may have given you a gift of teaching. Have you been teaching?"

I was always afraid of that gift because I knew myself well

enough. I had been a Christian for only six years or so, and I knew I could easily do it for the wrong motives. But I remember that moment when Bill walked in my office. I remember where I was sitting and how he stood, and it's really cool.

DAVE: So you developed as a speaker from there?

LEE: I had done some speaking in high school—some competitions and things—but I'd not been trained. Bill said to me, "I get a lot of speaking requests that I can't do. Would you be interested in doing some of those? If you are, I'll coach you." So the first church I spoke at is in Kokomo, Indiana. There were about eighty people there. I did my best and then gave the tape to Bill. He listened to it and gave me some ideas and critique. I did that for maybe a year or two—speaking in little churches periodically and trying to learn and grow with Bill mentoring me.

DAVE: Were any others pouring into you at that time?

LEE: Mark Mittelberg, whose degree is in philosophy and religion, was mentoring me for two years in systematic theology. Of course I had a lot of the apologetic stuff because that's how I came to Christ. Then Bill would have me do what we called "Scripture slots" at the Willow service—probably six-minute little segments between a drama and a song. I went from there.

DAVE: Who are some communicators that have influenced your style?

LEE: I'm not a great classroom learner. I learn by watching, applying something to my life, and trying it. I learned to write as a journalist because I would read the Chicago Tribune in the morning and the Chicago Daily News that my dad would bring home every afternoon. Then I sat under Bill Hybels' teaching as a congregant of Willow Creek for many years before I ever spoke, just soaking it in. He's by far and away my greatest influence. He is the most relevant communicator. He's just phenomenally gifted.

Rick Warren has helped me in terms of structuring messages. In a seminar I teach called "Preaching to the Unchurched," I say, "The best structure for a message is the best structure for a message." In other words, do anything that works! That's how I learned, but watching Rick added sharpness and definition to my preaching in terms of organizational structure.

DAVE: Describe your communication style. If somebody had never heard you before, how would you characterize it?

LEE: That's a tough question. If I'm excited about something, then I'm an enthusiastic and passionate communicator. I love storytelling because of my journalism background. I want the stories to be completely factual. But I like to tell stories; I learn through stories.

> "My biggest fear is not connecting— talking about a topic they don't care about. I want to be relevant."

In our course "Contagious Christianity," we talk about six different styles of evangelism. One of them is "testimonial," and one of them is "intellectual." In terms of my personal evangelism, I tend to wed those two. I tell my story of coming to Christ and how that was an intellectual journey, so I tell the evidence that I found convincing. Bill is a great storyteller in a different way from me. He tells personal stories, but I'm a little more journalistic.

DAVE: How do you prepare differently when you're writing than when you're speaking?

LEE: I approach them fairly similarly. I do a lot of research until I get to a point where I just say, "That's it! I'm gonna write this thing!" Then I sit down and write it differently for a spoken message versus a printed message. I'm very audience conscious. My biggest fear is not connecting—talking about a topic they don't care about. I want to be relevant. So since most of my messages are targeted toward seekers, I keep my brother in mind.

My older brother is an atheist. I love him. He's a great guy, very creative, fun, and brilliant. And when I'm writing a message, I'm writing for him. I've tried to reach out to him many times, but we've gotten into some arguments—we got into a shouting match at Christmas once. He's really as far from God as I was when I was an atheist, and that's very far.

The third message I ever did was called "The Adventure of Christianity." I remember fumbling my way through and thinking, "How do I do this?" Then I said, "Wait a minute! If I can write a conversation for my brother and just talk to Ray, then I would reach all kinds of other people just like him." So I remember writing this first point: "Why is Christianity an adventure? Christianity is great… blah, blah, blah…" Then I thought, "OK, what would Ray say to that?" I know exactly what he'd say because I talk with him, I love him, I know what he thinks. So I pick up my pen and write, "I know some of you are thinking, 'What about blah, blah, blah?' Let me tell you what the Bible would say about that."

So I just wrote the message for Ray. And you know what? He came to that one—it may be the only one…

It's hard for me to reach and relate to a faceless mass of people. What are their needs, you know? I'm better one-on-one. So Ray is the person I keep in mind. He's the one I write the message for, knowing that if I reach him, I just may reach thousands.

DAVE: What are the biggest challenges to overcome with your natural style, and how do you compensate for them?

LEE: Bill was constantly and relentlessly coaching me on this. Just before I would go up to speak, he would say, "Shorten it. Keep it tight." I challenge you to find anyone in the world who is a tighter communicator than Bill Hybels. Every word counts with him. Especially early on, I would give all this extraneous detail mixed with enthusiasm, and a story that should have taken three minutes would last for eight—and I would lose my audience. Bill kept telling me, "The more you prune the tree, the more powerful it's going to grow." So I manuscript every message word-for-word and literally write out every sentence. It keeps me from being redundant and forces me to think through new language. It causes me to come up with word images I wouldn't have otherwise.

It's hard work to force yourself to manuscript. When I'm speaking, I don't generally read the manuscript—especially the stories. But the discipline of having sat down and written and edited the message very carefully is extremely beneficial. I'm an editor, so I spend twice as much time editing as writing. Then when I tell it, it's imprinted pretty well.

I also will give the manuscript to Mark Mittelberg, and Mark reads all my messages. He's one of the best editors, and he'll make little suggestions that make the manuscript better.

But I can't do what my preacher friends Brad Johnson and Bob Russell used to do—work in community on messages. Message preparation is a very private thing to me. I can't let anyone in on that. It's God and me, and it's just very personal. James Thurber, the writer, would never show anyone his rough drafts.

DAVE: Do you enjoy speaking?

LEE: I don't know if this has to do with my style or not, but I'm still a reluctant speaker. Rarely do I feel like it all comes together, like all the cylinders are hitting. And that's why I don't know if I truly have that gift or not. I don't *need* to preach. I wouldn't care if God said to me, "Lee, you're never going to preach again." It really wouldn't bother me one bit. Some people are just wired to speak on a regular basis. If you gave me the option of canceling any given speaking engagement five minutes beforehand, I would virtually always take it. If you asked me to choose between sitting in a room writing or speaking, I would always choose the writing.

DAVE: Some of that may be due to your style. You have such a passion to prove on paper what you believe so that people can come back to it again and again as they wrestle with making a decision.

LEE: Also, there's a mantle, a weight, a responsibility in preaching that I take very seriously. There are times, especially evangelistically, when God comes through and you see results and it's worth it. But I'm not a week-in, week-out preacher. I'm not wired that way. I'm a writer who preaches.

DAVE: What goals do you have every time you speak or write?

LEE: My goal is always evangelism. It's always winning people to Christ. That's one reason I don't preach week in and week out. I don't care to preach about other things; they're not my passion areas. My number one thought is to see people come to Christ, so I'm kind of narrow. I make no apology for it—I'm an evangelist first!

> "My goal is always evangelism. It's always winning people to Christ."

Lee Strobel is quite convincing. He'll do whatever it takes to get the gospel message to come through—even if it means speaking, which he doesn't necessarily enjoy and yet does tremendously well. No one speaks on evangelism the way he does.

Advice on Refining This Style

◆ *Create your own defense.*

Lee told me that before he wrote the best-selling apologetic book *The Case for Christ*, he formulated the ideas through creating a courtroom setting for a congregation. He first videotaped interviews with experts. For his presentation, he'd "call" the expert to the stand, then play a videotaped interview as though the expert was giving evidence. Then he'd stop the tape, ask cross-examination questions, then play more of the tape.

Sharing the evidence, refuting false claims, and defending the truth resonates with these communicators.

It's tough to keep Convincing Apologists from the courtroom setting. Something about sharing the evidence, refuting false claims, and defending the truth resonates with these communicators.

If you've never laid out a lesson or set up a sermon to follow a similar line of reasoning, you may never dismantle the non-Christian skeptic's worldview. Give it a shot. Create a proof for the gospel, and present it as a courtroom drama. Even if you don't convince a seeker, your preparation will serve to bolster and strengthen your own faith.

◆ *Keep it simple.*

Since many Convincing Apologists are highly intellectual and passionate about sharing their wisdom, they must take care to serve it up in edible portions. Most audience members will tune out verbosity, difficult-to-understand words, and lengthy expositions.

Instead, serve small portions of gospel evidence. Keep listeners coming back for more as you continue to gain credibility with small victories.

Shortly after baseball star Mickey Mantle had undergone a liver transplant and had begun what he knew would be a difficult fight against cancer, he telephoned a former teammate and lay minister to ask for prayer.

The lay minister, a little skeptical about Mantle's conversion to Christianity, subtly tested him by asking, "Why would God let you into heaven?"

Mantle simply said, "For God so loved the world that he gave his only begotten Son…"[5]

Ultimately, the simplicity of the gospel usually can win a true seeker even after decades of refusing to be convinced.

◆ *Transfer this style's techniques to larger audiences.*

Purists of this style generally set their sights on individuals rather than groups. While they'd love to see masses make Christ the Lord of their lives, they tend to utilize this communication style with a few people at a time.

As you work one-on-one with a handful of skeptics, hone your skills in chipping away and rebuilding their worldview. Then use what you've learned strategically in larger settings as well. When you employ this method from the lectern or the pulpit, you're aiming with the precision of a rifle rather than a shotgun. God can bring about a harvest of some who have waited for the moment when they feel challenged and intellectually informed of the evidence for Christianity.

◆ *Buttress struggling believers with God's Word.*

God's wisdom is always better than anything of human origin. One of the keys to apologetics is validating your words with the strongest possible evidence. If listeners believe that the Bible is God's Word, then continue to take them back to it. When speaking to the Pharisees and other religious leaders, Jesus always had an answer because he knew Scripture. He knew what his listeners were thinking and where they were coming from. He could address their concerns using their own texts.

But you must also recognize that many listeners don't believe that the Bible is God's Word, so for them, it is no evidence at all. To reach these people, the starting point is often an effort to establish the Bible's veracity.

◆ *Get close to skeptics.*

You'll never reap a harvest if you never plant a seed. Some Christian communicators seldom "reap" because they don't "plant." If your talks always are written with Christians in mind, then don't expect a crowd to respond to the invitation. Think like a skeptic, and sprinkle your lesson or message with the questions they have.

Lee Strobel prepares with his brother in mind, which helps him to focus on restructuring a skeptic's worldview. Matt Proctor suggests that Christian communicators put up a literal photo gallery in their offices of a handful of people they're praying for and hoping to "convince." My work space has names and pictures all around to remind me that not everyone grew up in a Christian home with two parents who are still married and who embrace the Bible as God's Word.

Such surroundings create a preparation environment that keeps the undecided at the forefront of your mind. As you write your material and then deliver it, you'll find that even if the intended individual doesn't respond, others may. Skeptics will relate to you as you ask the questions they ask, and they'll listen when you answer those questions in your talk. But be sure to answer them. Seekers eventually will stop seeking if they don't find convincing answers to their sincere questions.

◆ *Pile on the evidence until the pile grows BIG!*

Let me tell you about Michael, a thirty-something pilot. He wanted to know everything before he could believe and make a commitment to Christ. We talked over lunch a couple of times, and I gave him Lee Strobel's *The Case for Christ*. He slowly made progress, but it came to a standstill. Michael continued to look for some earth-shattering piece of evidence. He waited, but it never came. He wanted God to do something so big that it would be obvious. I began to pray that God would reveal whatever was necessary for this true seeker to become convinced.

Months later, I saw Michael at church and could tell by his face that there had been a change. I asked him, "Is it time for us to do lunch again?"

Michael smiled and said, "Yeah, I need to give you an update."

That week he did. He shared with me how he'd begun reading his Bible daily to examine the evidence. He'd even begun meeting with a Christian man on a regular basis. He said, "I've realized that the Bible is true and that I had enough evidence to make the decision. The evidence came in a variety of ways. The fact is that since I started investigating Christianity and digging into God's Word, my marriage is better, I'm becoming a better father, I love reading the Bible, and my Christian friendships are improving my life too. Dave, I began to realize that God was showing me through adding up a variety of little things that became greater than any one big thing!"

> People can rip on religion, pick your church apart, and complain about the "hypocrites," but they can't dispute the power of a changed life.

Then Michael smiled and said, "I'm in."

I wish you could have seen Michael's face when his friend Brian baptized him. It was quite a sight. Michael has now become convinced and will use his study and research to become a Convincing Apologist.

In your efforts to convince unbelievers to come to faith, remember the words found in Jeremiah 29:13: "You will seek me and find me when you seek me with all your heart."

◆ *Share your story.*

Some of the strongest apologetic material will not come from a thick reference book. Your testimony can be powerful. It may not be dramatic or earth shattering but—please catch this—it doesn't have to be! What you share about your personal spiritual journey doesn't need to be flashy; it just needs to be true. People can rip on religion, pick your church apart, and complain about the "hypocrites," but they can't dispute the power of a changed life.

◆ *Strive to win souls, not arguments.*

My father had a professor in Bible college who once said, "When it comes to my Christianity, I've never had to apologize for my *position*, but I have had to apologize for my *disposition*." Regardless of your style or temperament, you can probably relate to that statement. The goal is not to be the debate champion; it's to lead people to a relationship with Christ.

◆ Aim for the heart after you reach the head.

If you're not a careful Convincing Apologist, you may stop short of the goal. It's very natural for these communicators to impart "just the facts"—and that's it. In order for the gospel to take root, it must at some point head south eighteen inches to the heart. I'm not necessarily advocating some emotional response, but a balanced gospel message addresses a change in a person's heart as well as the head.

◆ Branch out in your styles.

People become convinced through different means and methods. What seems to be irrefutable evidence to one person may not hold water with someone else. If there's only one string on the guitar, the tune grows old quite quickly. Make certain you utilize a variety of styles and methods in this book. The diversity will make you even more convincing as you defend the faith.

ENDNOTES

1 Norm Geisler, comments (Louisville, KY: Southeast Christian Church, Men's Bible study, 2000).

2 Ravi Zacharias, *A Shattered Visage* (quoted in Servant magazine, "Quoteworthy," Spring 1999), 8.

3 Stephen Brown, comments (Louisville, KY: Southeast Christian Church, Wednesday night service, April 2000).

4 Jerry Adler, "Unbeliever's Quest," Newsweek (March 31, 1997), 64-65.

5 Bob Russell, "Administering Generosity" (Louisville, KY: Southeast Christian Church sermon, 2003).

CHAPTER **7**

The Inspiring Orator

"Preachers face a bracing challenge: to proclaim the millenniums-old Scriptures in a way that never grows musty. We can say nothing really new, but it must seem new. Like a resourceful cook finding different ways to whip up a plate of meat and potatoes, we must proclaim the familiar gospel in unfamiliar ways, week after week (perhaps two to five times a week), month after month, year after year. Clearly, the creative demand on a pastor makes working as a restaurant chef on Mother's Day look easy."
—Mark Galli and Craig Brian Larson [1]

"My message and my preaching were not with wise and persuasive words, but with a demonstration of the Spirit's power, so that your faith might not rest on men's wisdom, but on God's power. We do, however, speak a message of wisdom among the mature, but not the wisdom of this age or of the rulers of this age, who are coming to nothing." **—1 Corinthians 2:4-6**

The Inspiring Orator speaks to help people *feel* something.
The target is the listener's *emotions*.
Think Kirbyjon Caldwell.

Similar styles: Persuasive Motivator, Engaging Humorist, Passionate Teacher, Revolutionary Leader

Words that describe this style: Stirring, emotional, touching, motivational, emotive, poignant, electrifying

You might be an Inspiring Orator if...
• you use your voice as an instrument when you speak.

Refining Your Style

- you have the ability to move and motivate even the early service crowd (better known as God's "frozen chosen").
- listening to a cassette tape of your message doesn't do it justice.
- you touch the heart more frequently than the head.
- you have a flair for the dramatic.
- you've ever wanted to give the sound man a little *feedback* of your own.

About This Style

Jill Briscoe is a dedicated Christian writer and speaker. She's married to popular preacher Stuart Briscoe. But she wasn't raised to love the Lord. Her family was tremendously wealthy. She grew up in an eight-hundred-year-old castle. When she completed college, she and Stuart surrendered their lives to Jesus Christ.

When Jill announced that she was going into some type of mission training, her mother thought she was crazy and tried to dissuade her by inviting Stuart and Jill to move into the castle.

Jill respectfully turned down the invitation. She said, "Mother, I'd rather live in my cottage with Christ than in my castle without Christ."[2]

When the Word of God is proclaimed in an inspiring fashion, that which is sharper than any double-edged sword *will* cut to the heart.

As I listened to Jill Briscoe speak, her phrases deeply touched me. Her words inspired me to hold on to the things of this world loosely and cling to Christ. Such is the effect of an Inspiring Orator. These speakers regularly deliver God's message so that listeners *feel* it.

Simon Peter also was an Inspiring Orator. He knew how to work a crowd. While he exhibited other styles as well, the Holy Spirit seemed to energize this natural gift whenever he spoke. Maybe that's why Acts 2:37 describes the crowd at Pentecost as feeling something—as being "cut to the heart." When the Word of God is proclaimed in an inspiring fashion, that which is sharper than any double-edged sword *will* cut to the heart.

If this is your stylistic preference, then your emotions kick in as you teach or preach. It's no secret what you feel passionate about

114

as you communicate in an emotive manner. But along with emotions, this style is born out of oratorical skills. Perhaps your speech teacher in high school noted your extemporaneous abilities, or maybe people at work comment on how powerful your presentations are. When Inspiring Orators open their mouths, people have no choice but to be drawn into the moment.

This style is similar to the Revolutionary Leader but is more polished in the delivery and more deliberate in the methods used to reach out and grab the heart. Also a close kin to the Persuasive Motivator, this natural preference is quite common for those who communicate professionally.

If this is your natural style, you excel at an unusual combination: the humility to prepare and the confidence to pull it off in front of a crowd. The combination of those skills is a great recipe for eliciting emotions.

Don't you wish you could somehow hear a CD of Jesus delivering the Sermon on the Mount?

Even if this style isn't natural for you, you'll need to be the Inspiring Orator at strategic points in your ministry. It may be expressed in obvious, flamboyant gestures or in a quiet, controlled voice like Briscoe's. Whether you're a natural at this style or not, it requires consistent practice. Otherwise, it will gather both dust and rust over time.

Jesus, an Inspiring Orator

Jesus employed a variety of methods in communicating. That in itself shows his oratorical skills. Don't you wish you could somehow hear a CD of Jesus delivering the Sermon on the Mount? Where did he pause? What inflections did he use to penetrate their hearts? How did he use his voice to inspire and captivate crowds? When he looked at some fishermen and said, "Come, follow me," did he shout or whisper?

Though we don't know about his speaking inflections, we do know that Jesus often used inspirational words that directly connected to people's feelings. (Just read Luke 12:22-28!) Christ also used repetition, as all rabbis did. On a couple of occasions, he was so inspiring that masses of people sat spellbound, listening, and missed a meal.

As is true with all these communication styles, Jesus is the best example. Even greater than watching his messages on DVD will be the thrill of looking into his eyes in heaven and hearing him say, "Well done, good and faithful servant."

Kirbyjon Caldwell, an Inspiring Orator

Our featured communicator can memorize and deliver the truth in compelling fashion. He had the privilege, along with Franklin Graham, of praying at President George W. Bush's inauguration. Though both men were criticized for praying in the name of Jesus, integrity demanded that they be true to their convictions. Inspiration is enhanced when the one speaking lives a life of integrity.

At the age of twenty-nine, Kirbyjon Caldwell was appointed the senior pastor of Windsor Village United Methodist Church. Since then, the group of twenty-five members has grown to more than twelve thousand.

This visionary preacher is known and loved for a variety of reasons. Not only does he preach at the largest Methodist church in the country, but he also is a gifted leader. Newsweek identified Pastor Caldwell as a member of The Century Club, its list of one hundred people to watch as the country entered a new millennium. His business savvy, coupled with his dynamic delivery, makes his preaching both informative and inspiring. The results of his ministry can be found in a section of southwest Houston that will never be the same again. But all of his accomplishments didn't impact me nearly as much as his humility did.

Interview With Kirbyjon Caldwell

DAVE: When did you first realize you had a gift of communication?
KIRBYJON: I don't know if I have it now—it's still evolving big-time. You come back ten years from now, and I hope to be able to classify myself as an effective communicator.
DAVE: Who are some of the communicators who have influenced your style?
KIRBYJON: There are several. The first time I heard Vernon

Jordan, I was blown away because he was as smooth as silk. He never said "uh" or "er" or cleared his throat. Then following his speech, he did a Q-and-A session. I thought to myself, "Well surely he won't be as smooth in this because he probably had prepared notes for the presentation." But Dave, he was *smoother*. He is very gifted that way.

The first time I heard Colin Powell speak, he was addressing a conference of hospital administrators. He had the crowd in the palm of his hand. He was very genuine and connected really well—a potent communicator.

Another great communicator is Dom Capers, the head football coach for the Houston Texans. What's so great about Dom is that it doesn't matter if the team lost by thirty points or pulled off the upset of the week. He always knows what to say. I am convinced that on Saturday night he must prepare two different speeches based on whether they win or lose. It's phenomenal to hear him talk in the locker room. You should have heard his speech after their loss to the Kansas City Chiefs. He did a masterful job of turning their attention forward to the next week and challenging them to demonstrate character. I would classify him as an exemplary situational communicator. He knows exactly what to say and how to say it in any situation.

DAVE: Tell me some words your church members would use to describe your preaching style.

KIRBYJON: I can only guess they might say, "Passionate and energetic, with lots of action."

DAVE: Do you manuscript your messages?

KIRBYJON: I have some notes I refer to, but I don't rely on them. I walk around when I speak. I have never manuscripted a presentation at Windsor or at any church or in any secular setting. Now, that doesn't mean I don't know what I'm going to say when I get up there. But if I have to write it all down, I'm in trouble!

DAVE: How much time do you put into a message?

KIRBYJON: Not enough. For some weeks, I'd be ashamed to tell you.

DAVE: Every preacher can relate to "not enough."

KIRBYJON: With some sermons, I've prepared and prayed and sat down—and then like a mighty, rushing wind, it just comes out. Other times, I actually get some pivotal thoughts while I'm driving or in a meeting or something. Then I make adjustments while I preach because each one of our services seems to have its own personality.

DAVE: Talk to me about your use of repetition. Is that a gift or something you intentionally work at?

KIRBYJON: It's a gift from the standpoint that it's a manifestation and an extension of God working through me. At the same time, I am cognizant not only of being a good steward of that gift, but also of the value of properly placed repetition. To be honest with you, I work on it all the time, and I don't think I do enough of it.

DAVE: You often lead the congregation in repeating something along with you. Is that a trademark each time you read the Scripture text?

KIRBYJON: I started doing that maybe two years ago, and it's sort of a tradition. I enjoy it—I haven't really asked them! But I do like to get the audience involved.

DAVE: What are some of the weaknesses of your style?

KIRBYJON: I think I need to use more stories to drive home the points of the passage. I've come to the conclusion that if you're preaching through the book of Genesis, you don't need to add stories because it already has so many stories that make the points themselves. So maybe that's why over the years I've developed a habit of not intentionally going after outside stories. But with some of the passages in Acts that may not readily lend themselves to exposition, you need to add some stories. There's nothing like a powerful story! That's why Jesus told all those parables. People could take those home.

Personal stories can work particularly well. The reason is that folk are nosy; when they think you're telling them something about your own life and your children's lives, they receive that into the nosy part of their psyche. If the story can help hammer home the theological point or the spiritual value of the message, that's all the better. But I don't do very well telling personal stories about my own life, and I need to do a better job of hunting down and identifying stories.

DAVE: What are some of your goals each time you step into the pulpit?

KIRBYJON: Let me answer your question this way: I always ask myself, "When this message is over, what do I want people to *believe*, what do I want people to *think*, what do I want people to *do*, and what do I want people to *feel*?"

My ultimate goal is for them to grow in holiness and the understanding of God's Word. More pragmatically, it's about them seeing the text and seeing themselves in the text.

DAVE: What's more natural for you—the delivery or the preparation?

KIRBYJON: That's easy—delivery.

DAVE: I appreciate your humility. You've had opportunities to work into your comments your relationship with President George W. Bush, but you haven't. That's a delicate position for a preacher, but let me ask you a couple of questions about it. You have the ear of President Bush. Why do you think God allowed that to come about?

KIRBYJON: Actually, I don't normally answer questions about President Bush. That's not something he asks me to do. In thinking and praying about it over the years, this is just something God has led me to do. I think it's part of being a good steward of the relationship.

DAVE: That's probably why he's chosen you to personally pastor him. How long have you known him, and what's your take on his communication?

KIRBYJON: I've known him about eight and a half years. He's a good guy. He came in three weeks ago and helped us raise a million dollars. He delivered a great speech. As we walked to his car following his speech, I told him, "There was a rock star atmosphere in there for your speech."

> "I always ask myself, 'When this message is over, what do I want people to *believe*, what do I want people to *think*, what do I want people to *do*, and what do I want people to *feel?*'"

He quickly replied, "Yeah, it's the office, it's the office." We started talking about something else, and he headed on.

I wrote him a letter the next day and said, "The folk who were at the rope following your speech trying to shake your hand and have their picture taken with you did not connect with the *office* without connecting with the *person* in the office first. And that connection occurred during your speech."

"If you're not connecting, you're not communicating."

What was so pivotal about his speech was that folk didn't just *hear* him—they *felt* him. They felt his passion and integrity. And he wrote the speech himself because I could see it was in his handwriting. He really connected. If you're not connecting, you're not communicating.

DAVE: You and Franklin Graham both prayed at President Bush's inauguration, and you both caught incredible flack for praying in the name of Jesus. Is that a true statement?

KIRBYJON: *Sufficient* flack, yeah. Introducing President George W. Bush at the Republican Convention before he was elected president would fall into the *incredible* flack category. It's all relative, you know. Had I not experienced that, I probably would have categorized the inauguration as *incredible* flack.

DAVE: How has God used your communication gifts to impact your community?

KIRBYJON: I think perhaps the most pivotal role of my communication style relates to impacting ministry beyond the four walls of the church. God has blessed me with the ability to cast and communicate vision, to encourage folks to get engaged around the vision, and to keep them engaged until those visions become reality. All of that begins with a word—the spoken word.

DAVE: Anything else you would love to pass on to other communicators?

KIRBYJON: This is going to sound trite, and I don't intend for it to: I had a professor of homiletics at SMU, at the Perkins School of Theology, who really encouraged us to *be ourselves* in the pulpit. Don't try to imitate somebody else. Don't try to step beyond yourself in order to be a vessel of God. Just be yourself, preach from where you are, and ask the Holy Spirit to use you. I think that's excellent advice.

I couldn't agree with him more. (Sounds like a good concept for a book!) Kirbyjon's natural communication style inspires people to take action. As is true when listening to many Inspiring Orators, he has the ability to light up a room in a matter of minutes. Time flies, and listeners sit on the edge of their seats.

> "Just be yourself, preach from where you are, and ask the Holy Spirit to use you."

Advice on Refining This Style

◆ *Put your talk to the "inspiration test."*
Kirbyjon shared four questions he always asks himself before stepping into the pulpit. These can provide a good barometer for you as well to recognize whether or not the lesson or message will inspire.

1. What do I want my people to believe?
2. What do I want my people to think?
3. What do I want my people to do?
4. What do I want my people to feel?

◆ *Let the Bible inspire.*
Make certain that God's Word is a big part of your message. The Bible provides the inspiration where we are dull. If handled correctly, the "word of truth" touches the head and the heart.

◆ *Memorize for maximum inspiration.*
Why would Inspiring Orators memorize lengthy sections of their presentations? The answer is simple: Because they can. Memorization plays to their strengths. If a singer has incredible vocal range, she selects a song that accentuates those gifts. If a tennis player has long arms, he's more apt to rush the net. If you have the oratorical skill to memorize and still *deliver your words conversationally*, then take advantage of it. The extra eye contact engages the listeners and also sets them at ease. The audience

feels that the speaker is confident enough to deliver in that particular setting, so they're more deeply impacted. Memorization is perhaps the quickest and most effective way to convey such confidence to the audience. It shows preparation and exudes poise. That's why Inspiring Orators play to their strength and utilize their memorization skills.

If you have the oratorical skill to memorize and still *deliver your words conversationally*, then take advantage of it.

Some time ago our church hired a young man, Kyle Idleman, to join our preaching team.[3] Kyle is an excellent preacher who has an incredible gift of memorizing a manuscript and then delivering it in a conversational fashion. For weeks after Kyle joined the team, church members said to Bob Russell and me, "You all never memorize your sermons. Kyle is phenomenal." Frankly, we were starting to get sick of all the comments!

Then Hall of Fame basketball coach Denny Crum, a member of our church, invited Bob to go to a college basketball tournament in Indianapolis. Coach Crum wanted to introduce Bob to his mentor, coaching legend John Wooden. Going to the tournament would mean Bob would miss Kyle's Saturday night sermon. Bob said, "At least this way I won't have to hear people on Saturday night say to me, 'We love Kyle because he doesn't use notes.'"

When Bob told Kyle about the opportunity, Kyle replied, "That's great. Tell Coach Wooden I said, 'hi.'"

Surprised, Bob said, "You know John Wooden?"

Kyle explained, "He used to attend the church where I was on staff outside of Los Angeles. We became friends, and he was kind of a mentor to me."

The basketball game was on national television, and we who were watching at home could actually see Denny Crum introducing Bob to Coach Wooden. But we didn't hear the conversation that took place afterward. Bob said to Coach Wooden, "Hey, Kyle Idleman works on our staff, and he told me to tell you 'hi.'"

Without missing a beat, Coach Wooden said, "Kyle Idleman—he's the only preacher we ever had who never used any notes."

Bob later told that story to our congregation and said, "I

should have stayed in Louisville that night!"

Some can memorize lengthy texts, and some can't. Memory is like a muscle; the more it's used and stretched, the more it improves. Those who choose to develop this gift and work diligently in pursuing it will reap the rewards of better eye contact and more engaged listeners.

◆ Bring your audience to tears or cheers.

Connect with your listeners through emotions. A variety of ways are available to accomplish this; a short list includes poignant stories, bold stands on issues, eye contact, voice inflection, and anything that has to do with children or family or death.

The bottom line is that sincerity and transparency can bring people to tears, and courageous passion can bring people to cheers. Be careful, though. Tears and cheers are not the *goal* of your communication. Rather, those responses are often *byproducts* of the Inspiring Orator.

◆ Cast vision to inspire your listeners.

Whenever you focus on the future and what it can be, you have the opportunity to inspire. Inspiration is contagious, so members of your small group or church will want to be included in the vision. As you lead them through changes, you'll discover that information can lead to inspiration. Your words can serve as a catalyst for people to reach their potential.

◆ Use your voice to your advantage.

Like a musical instrument, your vocal cords can run the range in an effort to connect with the heart. At times the message calls for shouting; other times, it demands whispering. If the voice inflections are truly heartfelt rather than manipulative, they can pull at listeners' heartstrings. If you are genuine, your voice can penetrate a hardened heart—that's emotion without emotionalism. Listen to how Kirbyjon Caldwell does it in the audio clip we included in the accompanying CD.

But be careful. If the congregation feels like you are

manipulating them with your mannerisms or inflections, they'll tune you out like a weak radio signal. Too much vocal variance can actually detract from the respectability you've earned as a communicator. It can cheapen your influence and cause people to hear and see you as a caricature or a *Saturday Night Live* character.

◆ *Use the tricks of the trade.*

God has blessed us with creativity, so use a variety of speaking techniques. Alliteration, rhythmic rhyming, unorthodox pacing, tearful conclusions, and effective pauses are just some of the techniques you can employ to inspire others. You are only limited by your own creativity and desire to turn weaknesses into strengths. An unusual cadence, for example, can hold your listeners' attention. The pauses inspire the audience to be more attentive and anticipatory.

> If the congregation feels like you are manipulating them with your mannerisms or inflections, they'll tune you out like a weak radio signal.

Radio commentator and committed Christian Paul Harvey shines in this arena. His golden vocal cords and unusual pace command attention. Paul Harvey speaks, and millions listen. He has perfected the dramatic pause.

Larry King interviewed Harvey and asked him about his trademark pauses. Harvey replied, "I'm asked that question a lot and I'm not even aware of it."[4]

After a conversation with Mark Mittelberg, I was further convinced that Harvey was unaware of the power of his pregnant pauses. Mark told me about a time he and Lee Strobel were privileged to sit in Paul Harvey's studio to observe a live broadcast. After Harvey briefly met these observers, they were seated across from him.

He began the broadcast. Strategically placed all around his table were different pieces of paper containing a variety of illustrations. Harvey intermittently would reach down, grab a different sheet of paper, and read from it. Mark remembers, "Then Paul Harvey said, 'Mark…' followed by a long pause as he looked in my direction. I thought, 'Oh no! He's forgotten my last name and, for some reason, wants to make a comment about me.' I was so close to saying 'Mittelberg,' when suddenly his hand swooped down and grabbed a piece of paper right in front of me. He said, '...Thompson of Cincinnati, Ohio' and began to read."

If you'd like to grow as a Relevant Illustrator or Inspiring Orator, Harvey's material and delivery could help you. Listen to his broadcast and jot down notes. His stories and careful wording provide a daily communication class for perceptive wanna-be communicators. Also listen to the audio CD that accompanies this book to hear various featured communicators employ pauses and other such techniques to their advantage.

◆ Involve the audience in your presentation.

Asking your listeners to respond in some fashion during your talk engages them. You may have them repeat after you as Joel Osteen and Kirbyjon Caldwell do. Another technique is to have groups read the text out loud with you. Saying something in addition to hearing it also improves retention. Whether the audience is a large group or small Bible study, involving them pulls them into your message like a fish on a hook.

◆ Learn to say "no" at times to what comes naturally.

If your emotions are always on your sleeve, if every week you tear up a couple of times, then pretty soon the tears become expected and lose their impact. When you start to become too predictable, intentionally choose another route. The decision not to follow the ordinary flow can make all the difference.

◆ Don't measure your effectiveness by the emotions or comments of the listeners.

Some of your high school or college teachers were great at holding your attention. Their classes may have seemed great, but could you verbalize what you'd been taught when you headed home?

Your class or congregation may get really fired up and respond through "amens" and applause. But be careful not to read too much into comments like "You made me cry." First, the sermon may be a success whether or not a church member reaches for a hanky. Inspiring Orators can resonate with an audience on a variety of levels. Second, you're speaking for an active response rather than just some feeling. If listeners can't remember on the way home how to live what they heard, then quality communication almost certainly did not take place. The true measurement comes days later if behaviors change and attitudes are altered.

ENDNOTES

1 Taken from PREACHING THAT CONNECTS by CRAIG BRIAN LARSON; MARK GALLI. Copyright © 1994 by Mark Galli & Craig Brian Larson. Used by permission of The Zondervan Corporation.

2 Jill Briscoe, comments (Joplin, MO: National Youth Leaders Convention, 1988).

3 We have the only transgenerational preaching team that I'm aware of. As I write this book, our ages are as follows: Senior Minister Bob Russell is sixty, I'm forty-two, and Kyle Idleman is twenty-seven.

4 *CNN Larry King Live*, transcript of "Interview With Paul Harvey," January 30, 2003.

CHAPTER **8**

The Practical Applicator

"When I'm listening to a good sermon, there comes a point when I lose track of all the people around me. As the preacher speaks, I experience God talking to me about me. The time for explanation has passed; the time for application has come.

"At that point, it's appropriate for the preacher to leave behind 'we' in favor of 'you.' No longer is the preacher representing the people to God; he is representing God to the people...He's simply challenging each listener to make personal application."
—**Haddon W. Robinson**[1]

"Therefore everyone who hears these words of mine and puts them into practice is like a wise man who built his house on the rock."
—**Matthew 7:24**

The Practical Applicator speaks to help people *implement* something.
The target is the listener's *habits*.
Think Bob Russell.

Similar styles: Relevant Illustrator, Persuasive Motivator, Scholarly Analytic

Words that describe this style: Realistic, fresh, rational, logical, reasonable, hands-on, relevant

You might be a Practical Applicator if...
• you can take complicated truths and simplify them into lessons for everyday life.
• you're constantly aware of what a nonbeliever or seeker will take from any particular point or passage.

- you love to see listeners "get it," when the light comes on and you know they'll integrate your lesson into their lives.
- big words and impressive jargon are forced out of your talk and replaced by real-life situations.

About This Style

David Enyart tells of an overseas experience when he was paired with a mediocre translator to interpret his sermon. He writes, "This perplexing experience made me appreciate the frustration that listeners endure when they hear inferior preaching. The congregants gather, ready to receive the message of Scripture, but they are stuck with a poor *translator*, who either is unable to grasp the Scriptural message, or inadequately conveys that understanding. In one way or the other, the communication of the gospel is inhibited."[2]

If your natural style of communication is that of the Practical Applicator, then you're gifted when it comes to translating biblical truth to contemporary settings. To preach or teach in the early twenty-first century, the speaker is required to make a link to people. Seekers especially desire speakers who are able to relate. Practical Applicators make that link with a variety of age groups. Then practical application completes the package for their listeners, as these communicators excel in making applications through lists, phrases, succinct examples, current events, and stories.

J. I. Packer emphasized the importance of this communication style. He said, "Preaching is essentially teaching plus application...where the *plus* is lacking something less than preaching takes place."[3]

Jesus, a Practical Applicator

Jesus had the ability to apply his lessons to where the people lived. At times, the takeaway was so obvious that his listeners caught the application almost instantly. In John 8, for example, Jesus practically applied his message to a group of self-righteous men preparing to stone an adulterous woman. He simply said, "If any one of you is without sin, let him be the first to throw a stone at her." Jesus' practical application later came in the form of a directive when he said to the woman, "Neither do I condemn you. Go now and leave your life of sin."

At other times, Jesus wanted his listeners to make the applications long after they'd heard him speak. Remember the parable of the sower and the seed? Well after Christ shared the story, he explained and applied it for the disciples.

Regardless of the time frame—immediate or delayed—Jesus placed a high priority on practical application. He knew that without it, people would never leave their sinful habits and implement new disciplines.

Bob Russell, a Practical Applicator

Our featured communicator for this chapter is a farm boy from Pennsylvania. A year after graduating from Cincinnati Bible College, he came to Southeast Christian Church in Louisville, Kentucky. God has dramatically blessed Bob Russell's ministry. Growing from 120 members back in 1966 to a typical weekend worship attendance of more than 18,000, the church is still growing. Bob's credible leadership, integrity, humility, and preaching ability—week in and week out—make him the best preacher I know. His commitment to preaching the truth and practically applying it is unequaled. Both long-term members and first-time visitors say about him, "Bob has a gift of making the Bible practical to my daily life." It has been my personal privilege to share the preaching responsibilities with Bob for more than fifteen years.

Interview With Bob Russell

INTERVIEW

DAVE: When did you first realize you had some gifts in communication?

BOB: I never saw myself as a communicator when I was growing up. Once in seventh grade when I got up to read in class, my voice cracked for some reason and the kids laughed. It made me very self-conscious. For a long period after that, I would hyperventilate every time I was asked to read in class or give a speech. My heart would pound, I wouldn't be able to catch my breath, my voice would quiver. I'd have to stop in the middle of a sentence and breathe hard. So I just dreaded speaking in public. The last occupation I would have thought of for myself was "preacher." I wanted to hide, not be up in front of people.

In April of my senior year, I felt like the Lord was leading me to Bible college and ministry. From that point on, I was able to get up and preach. In Bible college when I would get up to give a devotional, people were very encouraging. But I think seeing results in my student ministry in Ohio—to see attendance grow from 75 to 150 people—was really encouraging. It was an indication that people were receiving at least something from what I said.

DAVE: How has God confirmed your decision throughout your ministry?

BOB: Probably the most dramatic example of his personal confirmation was a number of years ago. One night I couldn't sleep, so I popped in a videotape of Chuck Colson guest speaking here at church. It was great! What I didn't know was that a sermon of mine was on the same tape immediately following Chuck. So as I went to turn off the VCR, I popped up on the screen. The sermon had been months before, so I couldn't anticipate what I was going to say next. It was as if I was listening to it for the first time. The more I watched, the more I realized, "Hey, I'm communicating!" The more I watched, the more I thought, "That's not me. That's better than I thought." It scared me to death. I remember going into the bathroom at 3:30 in the morning and just sobbing, saying, "God, what have you done to me?" There was more of a gift here than I had realized. While there are plenty of people who communicate a whole lot better than I do, I realized at that point that I was able to communicate better than I thought I did.

DAVE: In doing these interviews, I've been hearing a lot of people say the same thing—that the Lord must be doing it because they don't feel like they're that strong at communicating the gospel.

BOB: I believe a good portion of speaking is an anointing of God. There are different styles and different cadences, but there's something that happens when God's anointing is on a person that causes people to listen. It's an intangible thing.

DAVE: Who are some of the people who have influenced your communication style?

BOB: I had to be myself because there was nobody I was modeling. I think it's an advantage to hear good preaching, but it can be a disadvantage to hear the same person all the time. If you hear somebody too much, you just automatically imitate them.

One of the first speakers I did hear that I really thought communicated in a great way was George Stansberry. He's an evangelist and was a super-dynamic speaker. Listening to him was the first time I'd heard a preacher and had understood every word. He was the first speaker I heard that used stories and captivated attention. He had these sweeping gestures and this deep, resonant voice. I wanted to be like George Stansberry when I first started even though I'd only heard him four or five times. Well, today I speak in a way that's just the opposite of George Stansberry.

> "I believe a good portion of speaking is an anointing of God."

Probably the first speaker I heard that used different cadences and tempos was Don Lonie. He wasn't a shouter, but he'd pause or he'd speak faster or he'd change the inflection of his voice.

Both of those gentlemen impacted my preaching.

DAVE: Share some of the disciplines you've employed in your sermon preparation.

BOB: I heard a writer one time who was asked, "Do you wait to be inspired before you start writing?" He replied, "If that were the case, I'd never write." I don't think we can wait until we're inspired to write a sermon. We have to say, "This is sermon-writing time."

> "I don't think we can wait until we're inspired to write a sermon."

When I first started full time in ministry, I took a church that had been a weekend church for a hundred years. I was the first full-time preacher they had. They didn't have a study in the church building, so I had a little office in my house. At 7:30 in the morning, my wife left to go to work. And there I sat at 7:30 in the morning. Nobody's going to call me. Nobody's going to do anything. In Bible college, I'd grown accustomed to writing a sermon in four hours. I could write an outline, jot down some illustrations, and get up and preach it. So I thought, "What am I going to do with this extra time?" I realized at that point that I was starting a habit that could be with me for the rest of my life. At least I was perceptive enough to know that. So I thought, "I can go down to the drugstore and goof off. I can set up a golf game. I can watch TV or read magazines." But I made up my mind: "I'm going to go into that study at eight o'clock. If I'm not in that study at eight, I'm late. And I'm going to stay there till twelve noon, and I'm going to work on a sermon." Well, by Tuesday I was finished with the sermon. So I said, "Well, I think I'll read it over." And as I read it over, I said, "I think I can improve that a little bit." So I started writing out more and more sermons and going over them. I learned to do more and more reading.

That practice has stayed with me for thirty-eight years of ministry. I feel I have to set aside twenty hours a week to write sermons. I try to get an outline on Monday. On Tuesday and Wednesday, I read and write. Thursday I try to have a manuscript done, and I go over it with some of the other ministers on staff. Friday I refine it, and Saturday morning I read it out loud at least four or five times before I preach it. That gives me an idea of the rhythm and the feel of it. Since I'm not a naturally gifted speaker, if I don't go over some phrases, I might stutter and stammer over them. I'll still occasionally stutter and stammer, but not nearly as much as I would if I didn't read them over out loud.

So that discipline of just being in the office and studying and preparation and reading time has served me well over the years.

DAVE: Do you recommend your preparation routine for all preachers and teachers?

BOB: I'm not saying it's right for everybody. But I do think that blocking out large chunks of time is right for *most* people. There are some people who are five-talent people, and it just flows out of them. Most of us are two- or three-talent people who have to establish a discipline or be unable to communicate in a fresh way over the long haul.

There are two things to remember. First, God uses different methods. And second, I think people ought to stick with what they're most comfortable with. Don't be swept to-and-fro by every wind of new approach. Continue to improve and work with your own style. You can't fight Goliath in Saul's armor. You've got to use your own approach.

DAVE: What are some habits that help you think "practical application" while you're sitting in front of a computer?

BOB: First let me say why I think practical application is important. D. P. Schaefer, my home preacher when I was growing up, used to say, "Whenever you preach, always use a lot of Bible because that's the one thing you know is true." And I want to use a lot of Bible, not just my human opinion. But what makes the Bible come alive? In John Stott's book *Between Two Worlds*, he says the task of the preacher is to build a bridge between the biblical world and the modern world. If we can communicate the Bible in such a way that people sense that it applies to them, that they see themselves in Scripture, then the Bible comes alive. It begins to transform their lives and makes them come alive as a Christian people.

So we need to communicate the sense that "this applies to you. This is going to make a difference in your life. It's really important that you're listening to this sermon, and here's why." You've got to create a thirst in the people in the pew. Then they'll perk up their ears and listen.

Christianity should make a difference in every facet of life. By making the application to Monday instead of Sunday, we relate to where people live. We make the point that Jesus Christ is Lord of every day.

DAVE: How do you personally try to balance your message?

BOB: The ideal for me is about half Bible teaching and half application. I say, "Here's the point. Here's what happened to King David. Now do you see how this applies to your life? Here's what this Scripture says about people in the workplace. You see how this applies to your life?" Then pretty soon, the people in the pew start anticipating that. They start looking at the Bible through a different prism because they're seeing how it's going to apply.

That bridge to the modern world is over a pretty big chasm, so little examples serve as pylons. For example, I could say, "If

> "Christianity should make a difference in every facet of life. By making the application to Monday instead of Sunday, we relate to where people live."

somebody's hurting, somebody's in need, somebody's sick, you help them." Well, that's true. But I'd rather say, "Do you have a friend in financial stress? Then why don't you slip them a twenty-dollar bill anonymously? If you've got a friend who has a special-needs child, why don't you volunteer to baby-sit and give them a gift certificate so they can get out from underneath that responsibility? If you know somebody with a rebellious teenager, why don't you give them a phone call and tell them how the same thing happened to you?"

> "I think preaching has three ingredients: You teach the Bible, you *apply* the Bible, and you illustrate the application."

Those one-line examples do two things. It gives people practical things to do. Secondly, it opens up a whole avenue of illustrations that flow out of your everyday life.

When I was taught preaching, I was told, "You teach the Bible, and you illustrate the Bible." But I think preaching has three ingredients: You teach the Bible, you *apply* the Bible, and you illustrate the application. That's a big difference.

DAVE: What are some tips you can pass on concerning practical application?

BOB: Fred Craddock has a book called *Overhearing the Gospel*. His premise is that sometimes we hear the gospel better if we think it's directed at somebody else. If you go to church and feel like the preacher is singling you out from the pulpit, you're gonna have your guard up. You're gonna get a little resentful. But if you go to church and think, "Boy, he's preaching to somebody else," the Holy Spirit sneaks in the side door and convicts. That happens a lot at weddings. The preacher's talking to the bride and groom, and people are sitting there listening and kind of grinning about what he's saying. Then all of a sudden they get convicted about their own marriage and say, "I have to work on this." They've made the application.

If you can make the application to two or three very common areas, then the people build a bridge the rest of the way. Sometimes there's a big gap between where they are and where the Bible is, and you need to put up those pylons. Sometimes they need just one word, sometimes a phrase.

DAVE: Which comes more naturally for you—the preparation or the delivery?

BOB: Though I like both of them, the preparation is more enjoyable for me. That's just the way I'm wired. I enjoy the delivery, but it still makes me very nervous. I don't see myself as a dynamic communicator. I'm kind of a plodder as a preacher. I have to work so hard to keep people's attention and make the material logical so they'll follow it. That doesn't come naturally to me. I'm so dependent upon notes. So the preparation is more fun for me.

DAVE: You stay well-focused before and during your time in the pulpit. How do you do that?

BOB: Sometimes in the worship service, it's easy to get distracted. Or maybe your heart's not in the right place or your ego is in it. When those times come, I'll open up my Bible just before I get up to preach and read this convicting prayer, which I keep inside my Bible. Almost always it brings tears to my eyes. It changes my mood and helps prepare me to preach. I wish I knew who the author was. It says:

O God, don't let the pulpit call me to the sermon…let the sermon call me to the pulpit. Before I break the bread of life, Lord, break me! Wash from heart and lip the iniquity there…I want to preach, yes hemorrhage, under the divine anointing. God, strip me of all pride, all cleverness, all showmanship, and salesmanship. Deliver me from reliance on suaveness, education, academics, personality, notes, canned quips, and celestial clichés. Let me speak with the humility of Moses, the patience of Job, the wisdom of Paul, the power of Peter, and the authority of Christ. Lord, make my preaching clear, not clever; passionate, not pitiful; urgent, not "usual"; meaty, not murky.

May it comfort the disturbed, disturb the comfortable, warn the sinner, mature the saint, give hope to the discouraged, and ready for heaven the whole audience. Let self be abased, Christ be exalted, the cross be central, and the plea be with passion. May my eyes never be dry. Just now, Lord, take me out of myself, usurp anything I've planned to say when it's in the way of your message. Here I am, Lord, I'm your vessel! Amen.

That prayer means a lot to Bob Russell, and it's the way he lives and preaches. Working alongside Bob for the past fifteen years has taught me that effective application concludes with a practical solution. It's not enough to diagnose the problem correctly; there needs to be a practical explanation of how to correct the matter. Practical application paves the way for information to bring transformation.

Advice on Refining This Style

◆ *Serve hungry listeners practical applications.*

Years ago my wife and I were invited to have dinner at someone's home. We ate some soup and then waited for the hostess to bring out the main course. The third time the host offered us another serving of soup, it dawned on us that the soup *was* the main course. It's tough to serve something if it hasn't been prepared. The next day we compared notes with the other guests. We all had been confused, and we all had headed to fast-food restaurants after dinner to satisfy our hunger pangs!

> **Practical application paves the way for information to bring transformation.**

I've sat in Sunday school classes, worship services, and Bible studies where I was longing for the main course to be applied to my everyday life—but it never was served to me. Do you know why? *It's tough to serve something if it hasn't been prepared.*

Put in the extra time to help listeners understand what to do about the words they're hearing. How does it change the way they live? Application is the yeast that causes the sermon to rise, so your words will seem flat and incomplete without it. If you don't invest the time in preparing the meal, your listeners will leave hungry and may be forced to look elsewhere for food.

◆ *Choose your words carefully.*

A son wanted to surprise his father on his sixtieth birthday with a special gift—a genealogy study of his heritage. The researcher who compiled the genealogy said, "I've got some bad news and some good news to report. Your dad had an Uncle Harry who no one in the family knew about. He was a terrible criminal who spent time in the state penitentiary and was put to death in the electric chair."

The son exclaimed, "This is terrible! The gift will be ruined by what you've found!"

The researcher replied, "Here's the good news. This is what I wrote about Uncle Harry so as not to compromise the integrity of the work: 'Uncle Harry occupied a seat in a government institution. He was connected to his work by the strongest of ties. His death came as a real shock.'"

The power of the right word can drive home the application. Practical applications demand extra effort and detailed wordsmithing. It's writing and rewriting phrases and thoughts. Just the right phrase can determine whether or not the application comes through.

In my interview with Max Lucado as the Creative Storyteller, he talked about his extra efforts to enhance application. He said, "Last night at church, I talked about King David remembering the lion and the bear from his days as a shepherd. I had a lengthy sentence, and it just didn't work. So I went back and rewrote it. After talking about King David, I said, 'Forgetfulness sires fearfulness.' Those three words made the application that two sentences couldn't."

Craft the wording so as to enhance the application. If done correctly, your listeners will have no trouble making the connection.

◆ *Research the biblical setting to ensure accuracy in your application.*

There can be a tendency for Practical Applicators to spend the majority of talking time dwelling on the here and now. While that is very important, you need to find out the original intent of the biblical author and the setting in order to make the truest application possible. Please don't shortcut when it comes to Bible exposition. Practical application in preaching always requires some digging. God saw to it that his Word would be preserved for thousands of years. The least we can do is correctly handle the word of truth, as Paul asks of Timothy (2 Timothy 2:15).

Preaching professor J. Michael Shannon says, "If we help people understand the text, then they will appreciate...its relevance. I don't think you can make application to our time until you can make application to its original time. How can you know what it means today if you don't know what it meant to the original reader?"[4]

Your applications may seem practical, but if they aren't the message God was trying to convey, something vital is lost. The words are merely ours instead of God's.

◆ *Meet the practical needs of your people through the Bible.*
The best applications are always based on the Bible. Sprinkled throughout this book are references to the value of expository preaching. Isaiah 55:11 reminds communicators that the Word "will not return…empty, but will accomplish what I desire and achieve the purpose for which I sent it."

The best applications are always based on the Bible.

When you teach or preach God's Word, you are not alone in the process. The good news is that the Holy Spirit goes where you can't go on your own.

I had a ministry buddy who decided to write down what people said they needed help with. He says, "I ended up with a list of fifty needs. I literally tried to match a text with every one of those needs. I preached a whole year just on the things people told me they were struggling with."

◆ *Apply truth through timely illustrations.*
Some time back, I was preaching on the passage about a new follower of Christ. You remember the story of Matthew the tax collector who had a banquet for Jesus (see Luke 5:29-32). The guy didn't know any better, so he invited his dishonest IRS cronies along with his newfound friends who also followed this rabbi named Jesus. It's in that setting that Jesus answers the Pharisees' criticism with the words "It is not the healthy who need a doctor, but the sick."

Jesus always had a way of making sinners feel comfortable and the pseudo-pious and hypocritically super-religious feel uncomfortable.

Here's the illustration I used to ensure that the application came through:

Our family's prayers were answered when one of my brothers-in-law and his family recommitted themselves to the Lord. I'll never forget the next Christmas. They threw a big Christmas party and invited some relatives and some friends from their "party animal" days. After a couple of hours, my sister-in-law, Lisa, got everybody quiet so she could read a book to them.

She then read a children's folk tale about three young trees that dreamt of what they would be when they grew up. The story concludes with each tree being used by God in a big way—as the manger in which Jesus lay, as a boat on the Sea of Galilee from which Jesus taught, and as the tree on which Christ was crucified.

As Lisa read through tears, the guests became silent, hanging on her every word. Others had started to cry too. When Lisa finished, she closed the book and said, "I just want you to remember what Christmas is really about."

That would be the only spiritual message many guests would hear about Christmas, and some confessed that it was the highlight of the party for them. The party—and particularly the children's book—opened doors for us to talk with people about Jesus for months to come.

Who do you think had the most impact on the lost that night? The megachurch minister or the rededicated Christian couple who, rather than turn their backs on their pagan friends, chose to build a bridge to Christ?

When I conclude that story, I don't need to make further application. The church members have already made it themselves.

◆ Motivate people to listen.

Paraphrasing John Stott, Bob Russell said, "The task of the preacher is to build a bridge between the biblical world and the modern world" so that listeners' lives are transformed. You'll hear Bob doing just that on the CD that accompanies this book. It is sometimes beneficial in your introduction to hint at the application you'll make during the lesson or sermon so people are looking out for it. The hint becomes a built-in method to keep listeners' attention and to guarantee that they'll hear the application.

◆ *Occasionally leave some applications open-ended.*

In a sermon on compassion, I shared about walking past a home-less man who asked for some money. Two people e-mailed me and said virtually the same thing: "You didn't tell us if it's right or wrong! Should we give to homeless beggars or not?" I explained why I'd been intentional about *not* answering the question. I said, "Sometimes the answer is yes, and sometimes it's no—but I'd rather you figure it out on your own by following the prompting of God and sizing up each situation."

Don't always feel you have to dot every "i" and cross every "t." Being open-ended isn't necessarily bad with application—especially with boomers, postmoderns, and millennials.

Rob Bell, who you'll meet later as the featured Unorthodox Artist, says, "I want to leave you with something that you may not get immediately. The practical application may kick in ten days later or a year later. I think great preaching *begins* the discussion, not *ends* it."

◆ *Avoid the rut of always applying in the same manner.*

Practical Applicators are pragmatic and balanced. The good news is that you always know what you'll get. But it's easy to get in a rut where your applications are predictable and delivered in the same tone and fashion. Try some different methods. Try audience participation—shout out to them, "What did you learn today? How does this scriptural truth apply to your life tomorrow when you're at the club?" Or don't finish an illustration—tell them to think about it during the week, then finish it the next week. (Hey, that method works for television shows all the time!)

◆ *Don't always spoon-feed application to listeners.*

If your applications are always obvious, you'll create an audience that can't make personal applications throughout the week when reading God's Word. At times, be subtle and sneaky with your applications so that listeners arrive at the intended learning on their own.

After I'd done just that, someone said to me, "You know what

I got out of that message? I realized that I need to be more courageous in sharing my faith at work."

My sarcastic side wanted to say, "Duh! I led you to that conclusion by coming at it from five different angles!" Instead I nodded and said, "Really, that's a great application from that text."

Gradually you'll wean your audience of needing blatant applications and instead allow them the joy of making observations and applications during their own Bible study.

ENDNOTES

1 Haddon W. Robinson, *Making a Difference in Preaching* (Grand Rapids, MI: Baker Books, a division of Baker Book House Company, 1999), 94.

2 David Enyart, *Creative Anticipation: Narrative Sermon Designs for Telling the Story* (Philadelphia, PA: Xlibris Corporation, 2002), 45.

3 Michael Fabarez, *Preaching That Changes Lives* (Nashville, TN: Thomas Nelson Inc., 2002), xiv, quoting J. I. Packer in Dick Lucas, et. al., *Preaching the Living Word: Addresses from the Evangelical Ministry Assembly* (Great Britain: Christian Focus Publications, 1999), 31.

4 J. Michael Shannon, comments (Indianapolis, IN: Preaching Summit, March 24, 2003).

CHAPTER **9**

The Persuasive Motivator

"The most important persuasion tool you have in your entire arsenal is integrity." —Z i g   Z i g l a r

"To the weak I became weak, to win the weak. I have become all things to all men so that by all possible means I might save some. I do all this for the sake of the gospel, that I may share in its blessings." —1   C o r i n t h i a n s   9 : 2 2 - 2 3

The Persuasive Motivator speaks to help people *transform* something.
The target is the listener's *attitude*.
Think Zig Ziglar.

Similar styles: Revolutionary Leader, Inspiring Orator, Convincing Apologist

Words that describe this style: Convincing, influential, encouraging, inspirational, stimulating

You might be a Persuasive Motivator if...
- you'll use any delivery technique available to you in order to penetrate a hardened heart.
- you're willing to take a risk or do something embarrassing to motivate others to participate.
- your glove compartment is filled with tapes and CDs of motivational speakers.
- the words *tough crowd* are a welcome challenge.
- your firstborn is named Zig and is a girl.

About This Style

John Maxwell tells of a couple of college business professors who conducted an experiment.[1] Four monkeys were placed in a room that had a tall pole in the center. Suspended from the top of the pole was a bunch of bananas. One of the hungry monkeys started climbing the pole to get something to eat, but he was doused with a torrent of cold water just as he was reaching out for a banana. Squealing, he scampered down the pole and abandoned his attempt to feed himself. Each monkey made a similar attempt. And each one descended due to the spray of cold water. After making several attempts, they finally gave up.

Communicators are in the dangerous, powerful position of being able to persuade.

Then the researchers removed one of the monkeys and replaced him with a new monkey. As the newcomer began to climb the pole, the other three grabbed him and pulled him down to the ground.

After trying to climb the pole several times and being dragged down by others, he finally gave up and never attempted to climb the pole again. The researchers replaced the original monkeys one by one. Each time a new monkey was brought in, the others would drag him down before he could reach the bananas. In time, the room was filled with monkeys who had never received a cold shower. None of them would climb the pole, *but none of them knew why*.

No disrespect intended, but your listeners aren't all that different from those monkeys. Communicators are in the dangerous, powerful position of being able to persuade. You can move listeners toward legalism until they blindly follow your directions. You can mire them in the rut of doing things the way they've always been done. Or you can persuade listeners to follow in the footsteps of One whose persuasion was an outgrowth of who he was and is.

Persuasive Motivators speak with a certain energy. After hearing these communicators, a class or congregation is distinctly different—they've been "marred" in a positive way.

Persuading suggests action—not just emotion—as a result. True persuasion is the result of passionately sharing the truth and helping someone to understand the benefits of accepting what you're promoting. That may be the gospel of Jesus Christ or membership in your church or a small group—whatever you truly believe can change a person's life for the better.

The Persuasive Motivator, like the Unorthodox Artist, uses all thirteen communication styles—and whatever else is available—to influence the listener to life change and commitment. First Corinthians 9:22, written by that first-century Persuasive Motivator, the Apostle Paul, captures their spirit: "I have become all things to all men so that by all possible means I might save some." A unique characteristic of those who regularly employ this style is their willingness to adapt to the setting and audience. Paul did so not because he was weak or wishy-washy but because he was a persuasive leader.

Interestingly, more of the thirteen featured communicators consider themselves Persuasive Motivators than any other style (see "Featured Communicators' Self-Descriptions" on pages 14 and 15). Why is that? Gene Appel, the featured Relevant Illustrator, explained it by saying, "Those people who indicated that [they're Persuasive Motivators] are gifted leaders, and it may be an indication of their leadership gift and not just their teaching gift. Many of them lead through their teaching." Also, those with persuasive qualities may be more attracted to a ministry profession built on the task of making significant life change a reality for people.

If this method is not your normal one, then allow me to remind you that there will be times when you will need to broaden your horizons and be the Persuasive Motivator. In this chapter, you'll learn how to be more effective in motivating your listeners whenever you communicate.

Jesus, a Persuasive Motivator

Jesus was a Persuasive Motivator at times. Once he gently persuaded a man to trust in him for the healing of his daughter. He simply persuaded Jairus by saying, "Don't be afraid; just believe" (Mark 5:36). On another occasion, Jesus motivated a vertically challenged IRS agent to climb down from a tree and do lunch at *his* house! (See Luke 19.) Jesus persuaded a group of men who made fishing their livelihood to cast their nets just one more time. But it didn't stop there. Luke 5:11 says that after Jesus' request resulted in a miraculous catch of fish, the fishermen "pulled their boats up on shore, left everything and followed him." Wow, talk about persuasion!

Michael Fabarez teaches this lesson: "To Jesus, successful preaching was not simply to disseminate truth. Successful preaching was not bringing the congregation to an understanding of the truth. To Jesus, an effective sermon resulted in people grasping truth *and putting it into action!*"[2]

Zig Ziglar, a Persuasive Motivator

Our featured communicator in this chapter is a talented salesman. You might wonder why I didn't choose a preacher, but this man is the best when it comes to persuasion. Never mind that he has been known as one of the top speakers and salesmen in the country for years; what's really important is his passion to persuade and motivate people to give their lives to Christ. Zig Ziglar sees his calling as spreading the gospel in the marketplace. As he talks to tens of thousands of people who have paid top dollar to hear him, Zig will find a way to work the message of Christ into his presentation.

Zig Ziglar has inspired thousands of people through his tapes, CDs, and inspirational messages. He has served as the vice president for the Southern Baptist Convention and has written more than twenty books. The growing Sunday school class he teaches is a highlight of his week. Jean, who Zig affectionately refers to as "the redhead," is his wife of more than fifty years and is the love of his life. He can't talk for ten minutes without mentioning the Lord or Jean.

As you read this interview, you may have to make some shifts from selling a product to sharing Christ. But the principles and the plea for integrity are true in either case.

Interview With Zig Ziglar

DAVE: When did you first realize you had a gift of communication?

ZIG: Well, I can't pinpoint any specific moment. My persuasion of selling actually started out of necessity as a child. I sold vegetables and milk, door to door, after my dad died. There were six kids at home too young to work. There was a need.

When I worked at the grocery store and my boss would have some kind of a special going, he would say, "Now, we need to sell lots of these." That was all the motivation I needed. It was exciting. After I was married, I did direct door-to-door sales. It was really a question of survival for us because finances were always short.

DAVE: What communicators have influenced your style?

ZIG: The first one was Mr. P. C. Merrell. His sincerity came through so convincingly, and his sincerity was based on his integrity. As a salesman, he had broken all the records. He took me aside and told me that I could be the national champion. His integrity made me believe what he had to say—his integrity combined with the fact that he had been the champion himself. In other words, he set a great example.

No one had ever told me, until then, that I could be a great one, that I could be the national champion, that I could become an executive. Those were strange words and exciting words for me. And I did make a dramatic turnaround in my productivity.

In the next phase of my life, a man named Bob Bales—whose picture is also on my "Wall of Gratitude"—spoke professionally around the country. I'd never seen anybody have so much fun doing what they were doing. So the second ingredient to what I do was a direct result of what Bob Bales was demonstrating. He was a very bright man. His sense of humor was just so pervasive that it had a huge impact on me. One night in 1952, I decided that's what I wanted to do. I was twenty-five at the time. My wife and I went out to dinner with Bob Bales, and we talked. He advised me, first of all, to set some sales records. Then he said I should affiliate, if possible, with the Dale Carnegie Institute for the name recognition. Over the next three years, I did set some records. Then I wrote the Dale Carnegie people. I wasn't a Christian then.

DAVE: Describe for me your communication style.

ZIG: I would start with passion, Dave. When anybody of average ability does anything extraordinary, you can always give passion the credit. Cavett Roberts made the observation "Your belief in what you're doing is more important than the eloquence of the words you use to communicate it." So when I do sales training, I want my audience to learn that when they sell a product that solves problems and helps people, that sales process is something they do *for* and *with* people—not something they do *to* people.

> "When anybody of average ability does anything extraordinary, you can always give passion the credit."

Data from the Forum Corporation out of Boston explores the differences between the super-salesperson and those who struggle. The successful salesperson fervently believes in what he or she is selling, and the salesperson must have the highest integrity.

Interviewers say to me, "They tell me you could sell anything to anybody." I'll say, "They told you a lie. You just described a con artist." The professional salesperson would *never* sell a product that he or she does not fervently believe makes the customer the winner.

The spiritual parallel could well be that "he who would be the greatest among you must become the servant of all." As a professional salesperson, you go out there to serve.

DAVE: Any other words that characterize your style?

ZIG: When I speak, literally all I do is paraphrase the Bible, throw in some humor, and add some human-interest stories to it.

I weave a sense of humor throughout my speaking. As you know, I use a lot of one-liners. I tell the audience I'm like a cross-eyed discus thrower—I don't set any records, but I do keep the crowd alert! In public seminars, I have them laughing within thirty seconds. I found out a long time ago that if they laugh with you, they like you. And you've got to make friends with them before you can persuade them. I let them know in advance that they're going to enjoy listening to me. The bottom line is that humor allows the mind to spring open; then I can teach and persuade.

DAVE: What are some of the disciplines you've had to employ to overcome some of your style's weaknesses?

ZIG: For example, in a couple of weeks I'll be doing another Peter Lowe seminar with a talk I've made several hundred times. I'll spend a minimum of four hours getting ready for it.

DAVE: Even though you've done it that many times?

ZIG: Absolutely. See, I believe it's arrogance to think that just because I've done it all those times, I can stand up one more time and spit it out again. That's when Buster Douglas knocks out Mike Tyson. That's when an expansion team from Houston beats an established NFL team from Dallas. When the speaker thinks, "I got this sucker won...I got this one made...this is easy," the speaker stumbles and often falls.

> "You've got to make friends with them before you can persuade them."

DAVE: So you're constantly refining.

ZIG: Absolutely. I rewrite most of my notes because I'm just really gung-ho about the fact that information you don't remember is not really any help to you. For example, when I'm preparing and hit a snag—which is quite regularly—I'll go out and take a walk. While walking I'll ponder, "How can I use this effectively?" One of the biggest mistakes people make is that they don't think, "How can I use what I know?"

I mostly speak to big crowds, and [the organizers] are always kind to me and give me a significant portion—usually over an hour. Well, if I've got fifteen thousand people in front of me, that's fifteen thousand hours. That's a lot of people's time. I feel the responsibility. I do an awful lot of praying about "Is this message going to change a life? Is this going to make a difference in their lives?" And I'm careful with my facts and research.

DAVE: What has been one of the most defining decisions in your speaking career?

ZIG: When I started speaking, I had a good sense of humor and didn't want to tell racist or sexist jokes. So I created a mythical character called "this ol' boy down home." I would start out early in my talks saying, "That reminds me of this ol' boy down home." Then I'd tell a story. A few minutes later, I'd say again, "That reminds me of this ol' boy down home." Then the third time I said, "That reminds me..." the audience just started laughing because they knew what was coming. Then one day, through the course of time, I was introduced as "this ol' boy down home." I knew right then I had started down the wrong path. I did not want to be identified as a funny guy from Yazoo City, Mississippi. I wanted to be identified as somebody that would make a difference in people's lives. I left the humor in. I took "this ol' boy down home" out of it. And because I was getting so much response from it, the discipline to leave that out was intense. But there was no doubt in my mind that if I was going to be what I wanted to be, it had to go.

DAVE: Laughter can be so intoxicating. But you were making a slight adjustment to enhance your credibility long term. It's Christ who is exalted, and they walk away persuaded to follow him more closely.

ZIG: Today when I'm signing books after I speak, the two comments I hear the most are "I just love the way you talked about your wife" and "Thank you for bringing the Lord into this presentation."

One of the things I try to do with humor is to build a healthy image in people's minds. Often I'll say to audiences, "If you are somebody to anybody, you're somebody. And consider this: If man can take moldy bread and make penicillin out of it, just think what an awesome God can make out of you. You were designed for accomplishments, engineered for success, and endowed with the seeds of greatness. From this day forward, I want you to think of yourself as unique. You're different. There's never been another one like you." So that gets the laugh but makes a very strong point to be yourself.

DAVE: Talk to me about the pressures of being a speaker who people look up to and want to follow.

ZIG: When I surrendered my life to Christ, I made the decision that I was going to represent my Lord every way, everywhere that I possibly could.

DAVE: You know you're a role model for a lot of people. Does that ever make you nervous?

ZIG: No, because years ago I realized that I could not do it. I call my Sunday school class that I teach every Sunday an "Advanced Course in Math" because You plus God equals Enough. Actually, that's the message of Philippians 4:13.

I'm not trying to say that I've done everything right, because you've read my biography and know that simply is not true. But I do have a discipline that God has blessed me with—the discipline to study and read. I never go anywhere without something to read. Then when I weave in my faith to audiences, I always do it with humor. I'll say, "You know, I read the paper every day, and I read my Bible every day. That way I know what both sides are up to."

> "When I surrendered my life to Christ, I made the decision that I was going to represent my Lord every way, everywhere that I possibly could."

DAVE: When you're speaking or teaching your Sunday school lesson, do you enjoy the preparation or the delivery more?

ZIG: Obviously I enjoy the delivery more, but the preparation is what gives me that feeling. I've enjoyed the preparation because I've visualized what the response is going to be. You'll probably never interview anybody as blessed as I am.

DAVE: In your speaking in both secular and sacred settings, what's some of the thinking behind your frequent references to "the redhead"?

ZIG: Dave, you know God's blessed me with an incredible wife, and we literally are more in love today than ever. I'm trying to persuade people of the significance of their relationship at home. I want fellas to understand that their wives want conversation. Listen to what she says. I'll tell you this without any fear of error: Had it not been for that redhead of mine, you would not be listening to me right now. Her love, her encouragement, her support, her different intelligence, her different perspective...

My experience and research show that if standard of living is your number one objective, your quality of life almost never improves. But if quality of life is your number one objective, standard of living invariably improves.

DAVE: Let's talk about your Sunday school class. Let's think about the person who has to come up with a different sermon or new lessons, week in and week out. What goal do you have in mind when you prepare to teach a new lesson for your weekly Sunday school class?

ZIG: The objective is to make sure Christ is the center of the message. The second objective is to prepare people to live successful everyday lives. In the class, I teach how to set and reach goals, how to get up when you've been knocked down, how to develop a winning attitude, how to build winning relationships. I'm not really a Bible teacher—I'm a life teacher. But, of course, the Bible really is life. So my major objective is not to build the biggest Sunday school class in town. It's to provide teachers because that's the way you multiply and stretch the kingdom.

One of the reasons I love to teach is that it forces me to prepare and study. I generally spend all day Saturday getting ready for Sunday. I do little things along the way, but Saturday is the big day. That's my favorite thing to do.

DAVE: What are some ways you bring Christ into your communication in business settings?

ZIG: All the qualities I speak about are biblical qualities, so it can become life-changing. God's Word does not return void even when it's paraphrased. One of the things I teach in my sales presentations is how to ask questions, which is a key to selling. And then I weave in my faith this way: I say, "If you really want to know how to ask questions, get a red-letter Bible. Regardless of what your faith is, you have to admit that Jesus Christ was the greatest salesman that ever lived. Read those red-letter statements—those are his words. You'll notice that every time somebody asked him a question, he answered with a question or with a parable. You learn how to do that in the Bible. Then as long as you're in there, you might as well read the answer because one of these days he's going to ask *you* a question, and if you get it right, you get to stay!"

What a humble servant. Some uninformed critics might say, "Of course Zig can be bold in his faith with secular audiences. He's the best in the business and the most well-known." But what those individuals don't realize is that Zig Ziglar's speaking career was sluggish until he committed his life to Jesus Christ. When he did, he knew his relationship with Jesus meant everything and began to weave the Lord into his talks. It was then that he felt God begin to reward his boldness by increasing his audience. After all, God knew what people would hear if his faithful servant Zig was behind the podium.

Advice on Refining This Style

◆ *Stay motivated in order to motivate others.*

Sometimes it's that contest with the self that best keeps us motivated to preach or teach well. At other times, measuring ourselves against an invisible audience works. Legendary outfielder Joe DiMaggio provides an example of this: "Though DiMaggio's playing looked effortless, it was anything but that. He always gave his best effort. When a reporter once asked him about this, how he motivated himself to play so well each day, Joe said, 'I always thought that there was at least one person in the stands who had never seen me play, and I didn't want to let him down.'"[3]

◆ *Lean on the Spirit.*

Persuasive Motivators can encourage life change if they focus their own lives on the Spirit rather than the flesh. Just as you allow the Spirit to work in sharpening the rough edges of your life, the same Spirit can work through *your spoken words* to motivate listeners to make sweeping changes in their lives. One way to accomplish this is by inviting the Lord into the preparation process. I know you pray when you get up to preach or teach or when you're in the home stretch of writing your sermon, but what about praying earlier in the process?

◆ *Persuade with expository preaching.*

One of the biggest struggles in communication is planning what you'll speak about far in advance. Opportunities for persuasion may seem limited if dependent upon our limited intellect. You can overcome some of that frustration by matching up the needs of your people with Scriptures that speak to those needs. Digging into Scripture motivates people to transform their attitudes and actions. The power of persuasion is energized when the communicator relies on power drawn from the Holy Spirit coupled with material from God's holy Word.

It is not enough to persuade people to want to do something. The important step is to motivate them to the point where they follow through.

◆ *Motivate listeners not just to listen, but to respond.* John MacArthur says, "Here's a principle all preachers would do well to remember:…A major part of the preacher's task is to…press on his hearers their duty to obey."[4]

This is one way you can determine if you truly are a Persuasive Motivator or just a "wanna-be": Ask yourself whether you press for obedience or are content to give listeners information and then allow them to make their own decision at their leisure. It is not enough to persuade people to *want* to do something. The important step is to motivate them to the point where they *follow through*. The Bible may be the ammunition, but you need to be willing to pull the trigger. Inspiration without alteration leads to either frustration or stagnation, whereas persuasion coupled with motivation leads to transformation.

◆ *Increase your versatility.*

You have to wear different hats and adapt your methodology, as the Apostle Paul did in Acts 26. In this story, the prisoner Paul is given an audience before King Agrippa. Most jailbirds would use such a golden opportunity to plead their case for an early release. Not Paul. With the brief amount of time he had before King Agrippa, Paul tried to persuasively motivate the king to consider committing his life to Jesus. Talk about versatility! In one minute Paul's sharing his faith with his fellow jailbirds, and in the next he's trying to persuade the most powerful man in the land to become a Christian.

The King James Version records the king's reply: "Almost thou persuadest me to become a Christian" (Acts 26:28).

Paul did his best to persuasively motivate, though the Bible doesn't say whether King Agrippa made a decision for Christ later in life.

◆ *Transmit your integrity.*

Integrity and credibility open the door for a speaker to persuasively motivate. How is this accomplished, you ask? Through evidence of consistent faithfulness and honesty, especially over time. In your home setting, your reputation has preceded you before you even open your mouth. That can be good or bad. If your listeners sense that your words are coming from a pure vessel, your words will carry more weight.

Phony salespeople—those who seem to turn their personalities off and on—turn us off. The Bible teaches that those who will be the most effective in persuading others to consider Christianity will be the ones who are Christlike, 24/7. These communicators speak about life rather than delivering a rehearsed sales pitch cranked out like a recording. Consistency pays off in ministry and in sales.

◆ *Encourage change in your listeners.*

People are not motivated to change if they don't really believe they *can* change. Those who naturally communicate with this style use encouragement and knowledge to raise the bar. Encouragement persuades listeners, and knowledge informs them that their decisions are the right ones.

◆ *Capture and then keep your audience.*

Persuasion isn't guaranteed just because you gain your audience's attention early in your talk. While it's important to get listeners' attention early, their decision for transformation requires you to sustain their attention and motivate them through time to choose to change. Jesus, in the Sermon on the Mount, held the crowd's attention throughout before concluding with these words: "Therefore everyone who hears these words of mine and puts them into practice is like a wise man who built his house on the rock" (Matthew 7:24). Jesus was able to do this because he was trustworthy, authoritative, and compelling. If you are unable or unwilling to try to keep your audience's attention throughout the entire message, your request for a response will fall on deaf ears.

John W. Drakeford describes the dynamics at play in holding attention throughout your message. He writes:

> A preacher-audience relationship is in many ways a love affair and, like that experience, it is subject to great fluctuations. At the beginning of the sermon the audience may fall head over heels in love with the preacher, but if he grows careless and fails to maintain their attention, the congregation may grow disenchanted like a girl whose initial infatuation with an attractive boy dies when she becomes convinced he has no real interest in her.
>
> The question for the preacher is, how long can this close relationship last? Having gained their attention, can I continue to hold it?[5]

◆ Be humble and remember that God gives the increase.

Persuasive Motivators can begin to feel that an increased class or congregation size or a slew of decisions is the direct result of their talent and effort. You must be clear about the fact that while your communication skills are useful, God is the one who gives the increase. In fact, if you willingly acknowledge that, God may bring more people to hear your message because your intent is clear. If you don't believe me, just ask Zig Ziglar.

If the focus ever becomes *you* instead of the needs of the one you desire to convert, you've lost your focus. Zig Ziglar's motto is "You can have everything in life you want if you will just help enough other people get what they want." This is not a tactic or a gimmick. It's his guiding philosophy.

ENDNOTES

1 John Maxwell, comments (Garden Grove, CA: Institute for Successful Church Leadership, January 2000).

2 Michael Fabarez, *Preaching That Changes Lives* (Nashville, TN: Thomas Nelson Inc., 2002), xi. Used by permission of Thomas Nelson, Inc.

3 Taken from PREACHING THAT CONNECTS by CRAIG BRIAN LARSON; MARK GALLI. Copyright © 1994 by Mark Galli and Craig Brian Larson. Used by permission of The

Zondervan Corporation. Quoting William Zinsser, *On Writing Well: An Informal Guide to Writing Nonfiction* (San Francisco, CA: Harper & Row, 1976) 20-21.

4 Fabarez, *Preaching That Changes Lives*, ix.

5 Taken from HUMOR IN PREACHING by JOHN W. DRAKEFORD. Copyright © 1986 by John W. Drakeford. Used by permission of The Zondervan Corporation.

CHAPTER **10**

The Passionate Teacher

"When you think of teaching and preaching, the congregation needs to sense that there is something at stake."
—**Fred Craddock**[1]

"Get the word out. Teach all these things. And don't let anyone put you down because you're young. Teach believers with your life: by word, by demeanor, by love, by faith, by integrity. Stay at your post reading Scripture, giving counsel, teaching. And that special gift of ministry you were given when the leaders of the church laid hands on you and prayed—keep that dusted off and in use."
—**1 Timothy 4:12-13,** *The Message*

The Passionate Teacher speaks to help people *learn* something.
The target is the listener's *mind*.
Think Liz Curtis Higgs.

Similar styles: Inspiring Orator, Scholarly Analytic, Persuasive Motivator

Words that describe this style: Ardent, fervent, zealous, educated, convincing, compelling, learned

You might be a Passionate Teacher if...
• you thrill at taking your listeners beneath the surface.
• you're more intense when speaking than you are in your normal, everyday life.
• you're more attracted to the term *teacher* than *preacher*.
• your PowerPoint presentations and overheads are, in your estimation, the eighth and ninth wonders of the world.

- you thrive on digging into the nitty-gritty of the topic and Scriptures and then sharing what you've learned.
- you're more concerned with listeners' personal growth than with how well they think you did.
- you tend to prepare more material than you have the time to teach.

About This Style

When you're in a Christian college trying to juggle basketball practice, road trips, service opportunities, studying, classes, dating, and a weekend ministry (not necessarily in that order), you have to prioritize. I learned at the Cincinnati Bible College that each professor had decided how many classes a student could miss before it started to affect the grade. Discerning students would plot out when to skip classes throughout the semester and would always keep one extra should an unexpected all-nighter force a few minutes of shut-eye the following morning.

Believe it or not, for one class I never used any of those "opportunities of grace." Professor Sherwood Smith taught a class called The Life of Christ. Some twenty years later, his teachings still echo in my mind. When he communicated, his passion for the text transferred to me. I studied more and, in turn, learned more. Strangely, I became more interested in what this man in his sixties was pouring out to me than whether the girl down the row was paying attention to me. (This is not normal behavior for a twenty-year-old male.) I was entranced by his lessons as he taught clearly and confidently. *His passion for what he was teaching made me want to listen and learn.* Sometimes Professor Smith would quote Jesus—something I'd heard a hundred times before—and his voice would quiver. My eyes also would become wet as I realized from his teaching *why* and *how* Jesus said what he did.

Plenty of teachers had grabbed my heart, but this was different. Professor Smith's words seized my intellect. He reaffirmed for me that the Bible is true, that Jesus walked this earth for thirty-three years, and that I would never be the same because of that fact. Those teachings helped to validate in my mind what I already believed in my heart.

Such is business as usual for Passionate Teachers. They love to teach, and their intensity cannot be dampened. In fact, it's contagious. They're so compelling and informative that listeners become engrossed within a matter of minutes. They scratch where listeners itch with well-thought-out concepts and sheer knowledge. They long to take people's minds from point A to point B, but their zeal absorbs listeners in the teaching.

Changed lives often result from this collision of passion and teaching.

What differentiates this style from the others is an overwhelming ability to reach the mind through fervent instruction. There's no pressure to entertain—just a desire to help listeners learn. The size of the crowd is irrelevant. The opportunity to teach is the priority.

The power of this style is that these speakers convey what they know and deeply believe. Merely transmitting facts would be a passionless presentation and wouldn't impact the listener. These teachers stimulate their listeners' understanding of spiritual truth, and changed lives often result from this collision of passion and teaching.

Jesus, a Passionate Teacher

Everywhere you turn in the midst of Christ's three-year ministry, he is immersed in this style. He taught conversationally by the Sea of Galilee and at a well in Sychar. He taught emphatically when he cleansed the temple and denounced the Pharisees. He taught practically as he shared parable after parable to spellbound crowds. He taught sincerely when sharing with his disciples what he would have to suffer.

Jesus says in Luke 19:10, "For the Son of Man came to seek and to save what was lost." Those words reveal the force behind his drive to teach with such passion. He taught with a goal in mind—to help lost people find him. No wonder he communicated with such fervor.

Liz Curtis Higgs, a Passionate Teacher

Passionate Teachers are riveting. You are about to meet a woman who is just that. Liz Curtis Higgs wasn't always known as a popular author, Christian speaker, and Bible teacher. For years she ruled the world of radio. In Indianapolis, they called her the *Electric Lady*. In Detroit, she was the *Motor City Mama*. In those days, Liz partied as if there would be no tomorrow. What was her lifestyle like? When she did the afternoon show at WWWW-FM in Detroit, Howard Stern—who did the morning show—sat her down and said, "Liz, I'm really worried about you." When your behavior shocks the shock jock, something is awry.

Soon after that, Liz moved to Louisville, Kentucky, and became known as the *Big Blonde*. She did cocaine on her drive from Detroit to Louisville and was as high as a kite as she sat behind the microphone for her first show on rock station WQMF-FM. A few months later, she moved to WAKY-AM, where the Lord matched her up with a couple who had been Christians for only a few months. They didn't judge her or tell her to clean up her act. They simply told her they loved her and that God loved her. She found Christ at Southeast Christian Church in Louisville. Since then, God has used her humor to encourage, her enthusiasm to inspire, her writing to touch, and her communication skills to passionately teach the Word of God. She has presented more than fifteen hundred inspirational programs for audiences in all fifty states and six foreign countries. She is the author of twenty-one books, with over two million in print. Those who have read her work or listened to her teach may not even realize how God continues to shape her communication style. Her passion as a teacher stems from her amazing testimony.

Interview With Liz Curtis Higgs

DAVE: When did you first realize you had some gifts in communication?

LIZ: My father, who is now deceased, told me when I was ten that I had a good voice for radio. That was also the year I wrote my first (awful!) book, a full-length, Nancy Drew–style mystery. Daddy always said, "If you can write well and speak well, you can write your own ticket in life." Since my parents were not believers, their advice came from a secular, make-money standpoint; still, those were the two skills I decided to focus on. I also did drama in high school, did some community theater, and worked in radio for ten years.

Then I was saved in February of 1982. What I think of as my first speaking engagement came later that year when Bob Russell invited me to share my testimony. It was a Wednesday night, the night before Thanksgiving. My only public speaking to that point had been emceeing for my radio station. But to talk about myself, on the platform…well! I had never done anything like that. I didn't even know what a testimony was! When I realized he wanted me to share about my hairy past, I told him, "Nobody will ever talk to me again. I've been faking these people out. They don't know what my background is!" Most people saw me as a radio personality who simply walked through the church door. They hadn't seen me weeks before down at Phoenix Hill Tavern getting smashed. So when Bob said he wanted me to tell my life story, I was a nervous wreck. I couldn't eat for three days. (Too bad I got over it!)

When I got up to speak that Wednesday night, a mantle of peace fell on my shoulders, and I knew the Lord was with me. I spoke just five minutes, yet the congregation laughed, they cried, and they stood up. It was just one of those amazing moments. We all have them, and that was mine. I sat down, and Bob leaned over to me and said, "I believe this is what God has called you to do." And I said, "No way, baby! I haven't eaten in three days!"

Then the next year I went to the Praise Gathering and saw Joyce Landorf address five thousand people. And as clearly as God has ever spoken to my heart, he said, "This is what I have for you." I thought, "I am *not* up for this! I just want to hide on the radio." But God had another plan, and soon I was on the platform, speaking. It was not something I ever sought after; God sought after me.

DAVE: Who are some of the people who have influenced your communication style?

LIZ: Definitely Joyce Landorf in the early years of my speaking. She's an incredible communicator who speaks from the heart about issues people understand. I also became a regular radio listener to Chuck Swindoll. His were some of the first books I read as a believer.

Having said that, the truth is that you can get into trouble listening to a lot of people and trying to copy their styles. It became clear to me rather quickly that I have an off-the-wall style that's all my own, and that's what I needed to stick with.

Sometimes I get e-mails from aspiring speakers who write, "You're my role model, and I want to speak like you." I write them back and say, "Nah, you don't want that. Slot's taken. What you want is to speak like *you*." And even now when I'm facing a speaking engagement that might challenge me in some way—a really big audience or a mixed audience, which is tricky for this "girls only" speaker—my husband, Bill, says, "Just be Lizzie." And that simple reminder always settles me down. After all, that's why the group invited me. They asked me to come "be Lizzie." They didn't ask me to be Beth Moore. They didn't ask me to be Kay Arthur. Though Kay and Beth are my role models as two women who really teach with passion, the truth is that I'm just called to be me. And that's true for all of us.

> **"The truth is that I'm just called to be me. And that's true for all of us."**

DAVE: What are some of the challenges you have to overcome because of your natural style?

LIZ: I can be so passionate that I don't get enough variety going. I just keep hammering away—Bang! Bang! Bang!—until the audience is exhausted. Their tongues are hanging out, and I'll think, "Hmm...I'm probably coming on a little strong here." It's really bad when you're doing a fifty-minute presentation and you only realize that at the forty-five-minute mark!

So I think pacing is a challenge for me. I have to remember to pause, to breathe, to walk around, and to not say anything for a second or two. Rather than fill the air with sound, I need to stop and let the audience think about what I've said and apply it to their own lives.

DAVE: Has your focus changed over the years as you've ministered through speaking?

LIZ: A few years ago, God made a big shift in my heart about speaking. To be perfectly honest, I used to speak for a standing ovation. I wanted to make sure that when we hit that end— bam!—they were on their feet and clapping. Not because my ego needed it, although it probably did, but because that was the measure of success to me. If they didn't stand up, if my presentation didn't produce that kind of "yahoo" ending, then I thought I'd failed somehow. Then a fellow speaker, Layne Longfellow, said, "The very best response from an audience would be complete silence because then you've left them thinking about something important and not thinking about you." So now my goal is not to build up to the big splashy ending, but to end on a thoughtful note. I usually close with prayer because I want time for whatever God has said to them to settle into their hearts. My goal after I've prayed is to get off the platform so fast that they forget to clap. Or if they're clapping, I'm not up there to receive their ovation and can point it in the Lord's direction instead.

DAVE: What are some challenges in addition to pacing?

LIZ: Learning to be more contemplative, since I don't use as much humor now. I used to use lots of set stories to illustrate my points, though often the only point was comic relief! Now my approach is focused on teaching without the long, silly stories. I trust God to give me natural, spontaneous humor—the humor that comes from interacting with the audience—rather than planned bits.

It took me fifty years to figure out that I used humor in my life to hold people at a certain distance. So I've had to learn to put aside the humor and let audiences climb into my heart and see the broken places instead of the happy places I always wanted them to see.

DAVE: Take me through the process of how God has changed your style to more of a teaching ministry with humor as the sidelight.

LIZ: When I came to know Jesus, all I wanted to do was study the Bible. Then, because I was excited about what I was reading, I wanted to teach it. So I started a women's Sunday school class at church. My lessons were not meant to be funny; this was content-driven teaching based on Scripture. However, because I'm a ham I found myself adding humor to my teaching.

Then as I moved away from the classroom and onto the platform, my use of humor expanded. People heard me and said,

> **"I realized I never wanted to get on the platform again without speaking about Jesus."**

"You are so funny. Would you come and speak at GE or IBM or whatever? Of course, you really can't teach the Bible there, Liz, but you could put together a funny, motivational message and still honor God without going verse by verse." Easily done—there's no mystery to creating a message for a general audience. But as each year went by, I was speaking at fewer churches but at more secular places because—here's the honest truth—the money was good and I loved that applause. Thank goodness God has changed me in those areas!

He really got my attention in 1995, when I was invited to speak in Germany at a retreat for five hundred wives of U.S. servicemen as well as women in the army. When I sent them my press kit of information, they called back and said, "You *are* a believer, aren't you? We didn't really see anything in your material that said that." Now that got my attention. I answered, "Yes, I really love Jesus with all my heart, and he is all I'll speak about when I'm there." It turned out to be an awesome experience. That weekend I realized I never wanted to get on the platform again without speaking about Jesus. When I got home, I cut my speaking fees in half, began turning down secular dates, and filled my calendar with events for Christian women.

By 1999, when *Bad Girls of the Bible* was published, I was finally doing what I felt called to do in the first place—teach the Word of God using humor as a vehicle rather than as the destination. I'm very passionate about teaching the Bible now. To be honest, I did worry whether or not people would be receptive to the "new Liz." I soon found out that if God goes first you can be sure audiences are ready for what you have to say to them.

As a case in point, I have a funny story about pantyhose that I've told for many years—an eleven-minute, stand-alone story that doesn't make a point or illustrate a thing. It's just very funny—the kind of routine speakers call a signature story. Now it is joy unspeakable for me to put aside my "signature" and let God's signature be written across my speaking instead!

DAVE: What are some of your goals whenever you stand up to teach? Is there one overarching theme?

LIZ: I want to make the Bible come alive, which sounds ridiculous because it is alive! The living Word of God hardly needs to be "brought to life." However, people often see the Bible as a dead, boring, dry text. So my goal is to teach it in a new way, perhaps in a style they've never heard before. I do all my homework, using seventy-five to a hundred commentaries and fourteen translations—tons more research than will ever hit the platform—so I can talk about the Hebrew and the Greek and the intense stuff with authority. But when I see their eyes glaze over—whammo!—I'm going to have a little fun so I don't lose them.

DAVE: What comes more naturally for you—the preparation or the delivery?

LIZ: The delivery is definitely the easy part. Preparation is hard work. It's like writing. Writing is hard work. But it's in the writing and the preparation that I meet with God. That's when the passage comes alive for me, and it's so worshipful. You still have to put your mind to the task; you still have to open all the books, surf the Web, use the Bible software. But it's in the preparation that God speaks to me and teaches me so that I have something to teach others.

DAVE: Do you manuscript your lessons or messages, or do you outline them?

LIZ: I've never used a manuscript. That would be deadly for me. I speak and teach from an outline. The Scripture, though, is in my notes verbatim. I'm not going to guess at that! If I'm presenting newer material, I've got more info on the page. I may start with thirty pages of notes for an hour-long program; a year later I'll have fifteen pages for that presentation. I never speak without notes unless it's a quick message or my testimony, which comes straight from my heart.

DAVE: Is it possible for somebody to manufacture passion?

LIZ: Absolutely not. It's all about God. It's from God, and it's for God. Sometimes when I'm teaching, passion for the material and for the Lord overwhelms me and catches me off-guard. Enthusiasm—from the Greek, *en theos*—means "having God within." And that enthusiasm, that passion, comes from the Word. Someday I'm going to stand on a platform and not say a single word of my own; I'm just going to read the Bible and watch what happens.

"It's all about God. It's from God, and it's for God."

DAVE: You have spoken to and taught small groups as well as groups as large as twenty-five thousand; how do you get that connection with your listeners?

LIZ: A wonderful speaker friend of mine, Rosita Perez, once said, "The audience will feel what you feel." If you feel relaxed, they'll feel relaxed. If you're having a good time, you can be very sure they'll have a good time.

In the early years of my speaking, using humor made me pay more attention to the audience. And now I'm finding that paying close attention to what is happening in front of me also works when I'm teaching or doing more serious material. I look directly at one person in the audience at a time—long enough for them to *see* that I'm connecting with them—and we both recognize that brief contact. They might smile, nod, or offer some other small indication. I do the same before I move on. My theory is that everyone can tell when you're looking at someone specifically, and they're drawn in and feel a part of that interaction. It's also a way of acknowledging those who are supporting you as you speak. I'm saying, "I see you. You matter to me. Thank you for listening so closely."

My life verse is Psalm 16:11, which states, "In your right hand there are pleasures forever" [NASB]. This goes back to Rosita's statement: If I'm resting in God's hand and enjoying the pleasure of the moment, the audience will be right there with me. And what they're seeing is all God; it isn't really about Liz. John 3:30 says it best: "He must increase, but I must decrease" [NASB].

I'm excited because of the shift I've seen in the e-mails I receive. The e-mails after a speaking engagement used to say,

"You're the best speaker I've ever heard. You're the funniest speaker I've ever heard. You, you, you, you, you." Now they say, "While you were speaking, God said to me…" That thrills my soul. When you get right down to it, I don't bring anything significant to the table. I just do my homework, pray like mad, and show up. The rest is up to God.

Liz quoted Rosita Perez as saying, "The audience will feel what you feel." That sentence describes what ensues when a Passionate Teacher communicates. Liz excels at reaching people's minds through a bombardment of informative material. She desperately wants to communicate to her audience. Simply put, she loves to teach biblical truths that can deepen listeners' faith. Her passion serves as the jet propulsion to facilitate the teaching.

Advice on Refining This Style
◆ *Prepare, prepare, prepare.*
The task in this style of communication is not just to transmit a feeling; you are hoping to engage people's intellect. That requires a different kind of preparation from the other speaking styles. You've got to be able to give your listeners something they don't already have. As Liz said, teachers have to dig through commentaries and surf the Web and study the lexicon. Through this preparation, they find the golden nugget of information they're really excited about. Liz's segment on the CD reveals her own work and study that leads to passionate teaching.

Natural ability can help you short-term but won't sustain you over the long haul. If you're serious about being the best communicator you can be, winging it is not an option. Some communicators who don't prepare explain that their side trips are directed by the Holy Spirit. In my opinion, these excursions may not always be influenced by the Holy Spirit. I agree with former Eastern University president, Roberta Hestenes: "The Holy Spirit can lead *ahead* of time too!"[2]

George Eliot in *Amos Barton* says, "[Our parson] can preach as good a sermon as need be heard when he writes it down. But when he tries to preach wi'out book he rambles about, and doesn't stick to his text; and every now and then he flounders like a sheep as has cast itself, and can't get on its legs again."3

Those who choose to hop to-and-fro may be fervent, but their teaching could improve greatly with more order and planning.

If your communication has passion yet lacks knowledge, you'll never dent the listener's intellect.

Block out chunks of time so you can pore over material. Read a variety of commentators, both "dead and alive." Meticulous research and study allow you to speak with authority. If your communication has passion yet lacks knowledge, you'll never dent the listener's intellect.

◆ *Order your talks for maximum impact.*

While you may employ a different outlining method than Liz does, Passionate Teachers must be certain to support their statements. In fact, that's what teaching really is. It's walking people through the reasoning behind your point, explaining the steps you took to arrive at a certain truth, helping them understand how you got there so they can get there with you. The difference between excellent teaching and mediocrity is found in whether you succeed in taking your audience on the trip with you. In this chapter's introduction, I shared how Professor Smith made me feel and believe Jesus by transporting me back in time. Such journeys don't happen by accident. They are the result of careful planning, outlining, praying, and communicating.

◆ *Teach by building.*

Teaching is about building a body of knowledge. As you understand one foundation, you can build upon it layer by layer. You have to learn how to walk before you learn how to run. You have to understand addition and subtraction before you can understand multiplication and division. When your listeners share a common foundation with you, they'll understand the pieces you're adding; when they understand those pieces, they'll be able to get caught up in the passion for learning right along with you. Passionate Teachers get jazzed when they see the light come on through the expression on a listener's face.

I agree with Liz Curtis Higgs: Passion cannot be manufactured. But I would quickly add that while passion cannot be manufactured, it *can* be cultivated. The more you study God's Word and sense the urgency to teach that message, the more your passion can grow.

◆ *Be authentic, but not too authentic.*

I heard about a preacher who confessed through a sermon that after watching a Victoria's Secret commercial on television, he had an extreme desire for days to click on their Web site and surf the pictures. He went on to publicly volunteer more details of this spiritual battle. While you can appreciate his authenticity and desire to be vulnerable, he probably went a step too far. From that point on, his personal admission made some women in his congregation extremely uncomfortable around him.

It's one thing to admit that I struggle with making wise choices about what to watch and where to surf; it's another thing to let emotion and passion soil the pulpit. Our struggles and temptations should be acknowledged and confessed, but not detailed. Calvin Miller says, "I really believe that our own suffering makes our sermons very authentic. It's what you've gone through that's been painful that's matured you and made you worth hearing. But remember there is a little trick in confessing. The trick is to be careful how far you unzip the viscera in your preaching. You don't want to get it down so far you can't get it back up."[4]

◆ *Teach in a manner that attracts listeners to learning.*

Effective teaching embraces listeners in the learning experience. The language is even different, softer. That's why some audience members bristle if they sense they're being "preached at" as opposed to being taught. Here are a couple of methods that can help you grow in your passionate teaching:

1. Break up heavy intellectual material with illustrations and humor. After teaching something complicated, use illustrations to help your listeners stay focused, better understand what you're trying to transmit, and rest their brains. Laughter prepares people

for weightier lessons. Then you can go on to the next heavy piece with refreshed energy and refocused intensity.

2. Create bite-sized morsels of complicated points. That means choosing the three or four most important pieces of information that will bring your point to life, then making it simple and clear so your passion for the material is allowed to shine through. Sometimes I'll say, "Stick with me for the next few minutes. This is going to be deep, but it's so foundational for your understanding of the rest of the message." People respond to the challenge and appreciate the warning.

Passionless pulpits produce powerless pews.

◆ *Convey passion in your teaching.*
Who hasn't sat and listened to a humdrum speaker? Inside you're shouting, "Come on, come on, come on!" Ken Davis says to communicators, "If you are bored, then they are bored. I heard an illustration once about a man who was listening to a sermon. It was a good sermon, but there was something wrong. Although it was focused and had good illustrations, he couldn't put his finger on it, but he was losing interest. Suddenly he realized what it was—the person who was speaking was bored."

Passionless pulpits produce powerless pews. Perhaps you've heard of the church that caught fire. The townspeople quickly formed a bucket brigade to try to save the building. Standing beside one another were the pastor and the town pagan. Countless churches had tried to reach this man to no avail. As they passed buckets back and forth, the preacher looked at the heathen and said, "First time I've ever seen you in the church."

Without missing a beat, the man replied, "Probably because this is the first time there's ever been any *fire* in here."

You don't do your church any favors by blandly preaching the gospel. A belief system that costs you nothing will yield nothing. So step up to the plate and challenge your flock as you never have before. Although it may feel foreign, your willingness to step out of your comfort zone may fire up the church for the first time. In so doing, you'll touch listeners who for months may not have resonated with your natural style.

Bob Shank says, "*Career* is what you're paid for. *Calling* is what you're made for."[5] If you've been called to communicate the gospel and gifted to passionately teach it, then do so with intensity.

◆ *Passionately deliver more than facts.*

You may be passionate about the details and historical facts surrounding a passage. Make certain you temper your zeal to match the significant theme of the teaching. Insignificant background stuff pales in comparison to applying the scriptural truths to everyday life.

◆ *Look for ways to improve your teaching.*

If you always prepare the same way, perhaps by reading the same commentaries, you'll always get the same results. Try listening to a tape on a topic instead of resorting to your usual routine of reading. Shake things up by practicing your lesson out loud in front of a mirror. Tape your talk on a tape recorder before you deliver it, and determine what lessons or points you want to share with more intensity or verify with more support. If you really want to stretch yourself, videotape your presentation and watch the video before your next speaking opportunity. (May I suggest that you have a barf bag handy as this can be a rather sickening exercise. It's kind of like wearing a bikini: You can't hide your warts and flaws—at least that's what I've been told!)

ENDNOTES

1 Fred Craddock, comments (Indianapolis, IN: North American Christian Convention workshop, July 10, 2003).

2 Ray Johnston, quoting Roberta Hestenes, comments (San Diego, CA: Advanced Track Seminar of the National Pastors Conference, February 2003).

3 David A. Enyart, *Creative Anticipation: Narrative Sermon Designs for Telling the Story* (Philadelphia, PA: Xlibris Corporation, 2002), 83.

4 Calvin Miller, comments, (San Diego, CA: National Pastors Convention workshop, March 2003).

5 Bob Shank, comments (Keats Island, Canada: Christian Management Association's Executive Leadership Program, April 5, 2001).

CHAPTER **11**

The Relevant Illustrator

"When we communicate with people, we are again using outdated models. Someone stands up in front of a group of people and talks at them for thirty to forty-five minutes every Sunday, using texts and approaches different from the ones the people are used to hearing. These talks have no apparent relationship, connections, or ties to how they communicate with each other the other six days of the week. Again, what they wind up thinking is, 'This doesn't have anything to do with me; it's that religious game.'"
—**G e o r g e B a r n a**[1]

"I am the vine; you are the branches. If a man remains in me and I in him, he will bear much fruit; apart from me you can do nothing."
—**J o h n 1 5 : 5**

The Relevant Illustrator speaks to help people *connect with* something.
The target is the listener's *common sense*.
Think Gene Appel.

Similar styles: Creative Storyteller, Engaging Humorist, Practical Applicator

Words that describe this style: Fresh, eye-opening, important, current, informative, relational, pertinent, contemporary, up-to-date, applicable, significant

You might be a Relevant Illustrator if...
• you learn better from a story or humorous anecdote than from a powerful quote or a list of different verses.
• you scour current newspapers and magazines as a normal part of your preparation routine.

- you pride yourself on knowing who and what's hot and what's not.
- you're more apt to read USA Today than the Wall Street Journal.
- you love modern-day parallels to Bible stories.
- you look at your lesson notes and ask the tough questions: "Who cares? How does that touch me?"
- you're always on the prowl for good illustrations.
- you keep a pad of paper beside your bed so you can scribble down thoughts in the middle of the night.

About This Style

After studying and compiling examples of great preaching from twenty centuries, Clyde E. Fant Jr. and William M. Pinson Jr. concluded that "great preaching is relevant preaching."[2]

Their comment is simple yet significant. No one wants to go to a church where the discourse disconnects from everyday life. Preaching and teaching become, as Barna puts it, merely a "religious game" instead of the life-changing experiences God intended them to be. Relevant Illustrators communicate in a way that helps people see how Christ and the church tie in to their circumstances.

Relevant illustrators communicate in a way that helps people see how Christ and the church tie in to their circumstances.

Frank Harrington resonates with this style when he says, "The preacher must prepare, as Karl Barth said, with the Bible in one hand and the newspaper in the other. There is a profound truth there. If you're not in constant touch with people—knowing their hurts, their hopes, their dreams, the rigors of the reality in which they are living—you may find yourself in the pulpit answering questions that no one is asking."[3]

Relevant Illustrators value illustrations because of the way they can connect relevancy to the topic being covered. When listeners understand, through illustrations, how the topic is relevant to their lives, they experience spiritual growth.

While this style is a close companion to the Practical Applicator, there are some differences. Relevant Illustrators are more likely to speak about current events and issues. They tend to be more flexible and adaptable—for example, the lead story on Saturday's evening news may become the introduction for the Sunday sermon.

Matt Proctor, the preaching professor at Ozark Christian College who helped me develop the wording for these styles, read several chapters of this book in its early stages. He succinctly pinpointed the similarities and differences between the Relevant Illustrator and the Creative Storyteller, another similar style. Matt suggests, "A Creative Storyteller uses story in the place of propositional truth. For the Illustrator, the story helps *make* the point. He connects the precept to a picture. For the Storyteller, the story *is* the point. He believes that the story will accomplish what the precept won't. The Relevant Illustrator draws on common sense and everyday experience stories to make the connection. The Creative Storyteller may draw from myth, legend, fairy tale, history, or imagination. The Relevant Illustrator leaves people saying, 'Oh, I get it now.' The Creative Storyteller may leave people saying, 'Hmm, I'll have to think about that awhile.' For the Illustrator, the story is a tool and can be used when needed. For the Storyteller, the story has a life of its own and may haunt its hearers for days."

Join me on a journey to discover how you can speak in such a way to connect with your listeners.

Jesus, a Relevant Illustrator

Jesus was in touch with society. His lessons in the Gospels affirm the connection he made with people, and his illustrations pointed to people's common experiences. In Luke 15, he tells three stories in order to drive home one point: Lost people matter to God. In each story, Jesus raises the stakes. He begins with a lost sheep, then talks of a lost coin, then concludes by talking about a lost person. Everyone in his audience had lost at least one of those, many had lost two, and some had lost all three. Through his illustration, Jesus gave the audience the hope of a father anxiously waiting, scanning the horizon from his porch in search of his lost son. Can you say "relevant"?

Gene Appel, a Relevant Illustrator

In this chapter you'll get to meet one of the most Relevant Illustrators around. For seventeen years, Gene Appel ministered in Las Vegas and led a traditional church through some incredible changes in style. The result was dramatic growth from four hundred to more than eight thousand weekend worshippers. Now he preaches at Willow Creek and also has significant leadership responsibilities there.

Gene is one of the most consistent communicators I know, partially due to his ability to illustrate messages. The images he paints through his illustrations allow contemporary people to relate to the gospel message. He'll use any current event or other relevant situation to build the bridge to the seeker in search of salvation and to the believer in need of growth. One of his strengths is touching people's hearts even though they've been reluctant to let anybody touch them before.

Interview With Gene Appel

DAVE: When did you first realize you had the gift of communication?

GENE: It was probably in high school. I began doing some preaching at that age, and people were responsive and affirming.

DAVE: Was your father still alive?

GENE: No. I actually preached my first sermon when I was fourteen, shortly after my father died. I was a Christ-follower at the time and was really committed in my faith, even at fourteen years of age. But his death really gave me the sense that this is what I was called to do. I remember that a few hours after my dad died, my mom asked me to go and pay off a little bill at the convenience store because we were going to head back to Illinois the next morning to prepare for the funeral. I vividly remember the walk down that road. I don't know if this was God talking or not, but it was one of the strongest God-moments I've ever sensed in my life. I just really had the sense of, "You know, Gene, what happened to your dad today will happen to every person on the face of the earth. One day will be their last day. And there's only one thing that matters on that day. Are they ready for that? Do they know the grace of Jesus Christ?"

I think of that day as kind of my defining moment, my calling into ministry. I just sensed God saying, "If you'll trust me and put your hand in mine, I'll use you to help people get ready for that day."

DAVE: Who are some of the communicators that have influenced your style?

GENE: When I was a sophomore in college, I did an internship with Ben Merold. This was really my first exposure to someone who would walk through a book of

"Don't in any way alter truth, but encase truth in a way that they can understand it."

the Bible, apply it in practical ways, and illustrate it relevantly. My dad taught me to love the ministry, but Ben Merold taught me how to minister.

Then shortly thereafter, probably in the mid-'80s, I was exposed to Bill Hybels' teaching. The mind-set that Bill brought into his teaching was "We're communicating to unchurched, nonbelieving people. So base your message on the fact that people in your audience are not yet Christ-followers and are unconvinced at this point. View the message through their eyes. Don't in any way alter truth, but encase truth in a way that they can understand it." I was inspired from observing Bill for many years and from knowing who he is and how much time he spends with unchurched people. That was a new style of communication to me. Both Bill and Ben—in different ways—have probably most influenced my preaching.

DAVE: You're so gifted at plugging in illustrations and using them well. What are some of your best sources for illustrations?

GENE: My favorite stories—and the stories I feel I communicate best—are the ones that just come from doing life: stories from my own life experience, things we're experiencing as a community or as a nation, common things that everybody relates to. I'm not particularly drawn to historical illustrations from even thirty years ago, let alone a hundred—other than biblical illustrations, of course. I like current, fresh, contemporary things that everybody's living with. So over the years I've tried to keep pen and paper with me wherever I am. I keep a file called "hot illustrations." I don't file stories in there by a particular subject matter; I just write down things I observe that seem quirky to me. They may be funny, happy, sad, tragic, or engaging. Here's an example:

We were at a store near a cabin in Minnesota one day, and they were selling frogs for twenty-five cents each. People buy the frogs for bait. My girls wanted me to buy a frog for each of them to have as a pet. So I bought them each a frog, and they had a ball. They played with them and petted them and loved them. One day my wife, Barbara, was in the cabin with our five-year-old, Jenna, who was playing with her frog. Well, this frog had just croaked. Barbara said, "Well, Jenna, that frog's dead."

Jenna said, "It's not dead, Mommy. It's sleeping."

"No, Jenna, it's dead," Barbara said. "We're going to have to bury that frog."

So Barbara goes to the garage to get a shovel, and they go to bury this frog. Jenna's just crying and wailing and upset. Come to find out, Jenna's not crying that her frog died. Jenna's crying because she doesn't have a frog but her sister does. So Jenna asked if she could bury her sister's frog alive!

Well, I had no idea how I was going to use that in a sermon. But it was funny, so I wrote it down. Several weeks later, I happened to be preparing a text on Jacob and Esau and the sibling rivalry in their relationship, and there was my illustration.

So I keep a running file, and I might write down something I see on the news or an article I read in the newspaper or an encounter I have at a restaurant or wherever. Those things aren't that significant in the scheme of life, but God can use them to bring life to a message. They bring a relevance to an application that everybody can identify with.

DAVE: Do you just type out those "hot illustrations" as they pop into your mind?

GENE: I typically just scribble them down and throw them in the file. I've also kept a current topical file system since college. It's very crude and simple, alphabetized with different topics. But probably 60 to 70 percent of the illustrations I use pop out of the "hot illustrations" file.

DAVE: How do you decide which illustrations to use?

GENE: I ask, "What's the headline of this sermon? What do I want people to know or do when the sermon is all over?" I don't ask, "What's going to be the most humorous?" or "What's going to be the most moving?" Rather, I want to know what helps move toward the target of what I want this sermon to truly be about.

Then secondly, I look at the rhythm of the sermon. Throughout the course of a message, there are going to be highs and lows. There are going to be quieter times, dramatic times, serious times, lighter moments. So I ask, "What would feel most appropriate in the rhythm of the message in order to keep the listener engaged in the subject matter?" There may be moments in the sermon where you just need to lighten things up a bit because you've been dealing with something so heavy or something that's personally difficult for someone to wrestle with, and they need a moment to breathe.

"You have to be careful that your preaching does not primarily become about you."

DAVE: What disciplines have you had to employ to overcome the weakness of your own personal style?

GENE: I'm not a great extemporaneous speaker at all. I know that's a limitation on my part, so I have to be very disciplined about my study times—getting in early, keeping my seat in the chair, working hard on messages, and producing manuscripts. I have to think about how I want to say something. Even if I've got the right illustration, I can really botch it and lose the impact if I don't spend time thinking about exactly how I want to say it.

When I type a manuscript, my first draft is more often than not fifteen to sixteen pages long. I've got to cut material, say the same thing with brevity and a little more punch. That's a time-consuming, laborious process that I have to go through in order to say it the best I'm capable of saying it.

Also, I think when you're looking for what comes out of your own natural life experience, you have to be careful that your preaching does not primarily become about you. As John the Baptist said, "I must decrease, and he must increase." That's the fine line you walk if you're trying to be real with your audience. I find I have to be disciplined and intentional about reading and gathering information from outside my own interests and disciplines.

"To be able to illustrate relevantly is not that much more time-consuming than to not illustrate relevantly."

DAVE: Do you read much?

GENE: I try to read for thirty to forty minutes a day. I'll typically read from a couple of different sources in that time. I also listen to tapes, which I keep and listen to primarily in the car. I like to be fed by other people, and I like to listen to their communication styles many times.

DAVE: What would you say about crafting a sermon to the person reading this book who doesn't have the luxury of fifteen to twenty hours of preparation?

GENE: First of all, they still do life. To be able to illustrate relevantly is not that much more time-consuming than to not illustrate relevantly. It just means you have to carry forth a bit of a mind-set, an observance in your life, that others don't. So maybe you carry a microcassette recorder with you to capture thoughts from time to time, or you write it down on a piece of paper. You must try to become even more observant.

DAVE: Which do you enjoy more—the preparation or the delivery?

GENE: I think the natural inclination is to say the delivery. But for me I think the actual truth is the preparation because of the way I prepare manuscripts over the course of time. Are there times that you want a break? Sure. Of course. But you couldn't do it all these years if you didn't enjoy the crafting process. God led you through preparation for all those hours, and during delivery it's up to God to do something fantastic—something only God can do. I really believe the battles are won or lost during preparation.

DAVE: Do you invite the critique of others before or after the preparation process?

GENE: I appreciate critique all along the way. I typically don't choose sermon titles or series titles in a vacuum. I usually run them through a team of people.

DAVE: What about your manuscript? Is anybody going to read your manuscript for this weekend?

GENE: Nobody will read my manuscript, but I typically bounce thought progressions off people I respect. For instance, I did a Father's Day message a few months ago here at Willow, and I just sat down with Bill Hybels about ten days beforehand. I said, "Here's what I'm thinking about." And Bill had some excellent thoughts.

Here at Willow we have a teaching team approach, so we critique every sermon. The other members of the team, along with a few astute people in the congregation, provide some verbal critique and a few written comments. Maybe I said something that was unnecessarily offensive to someone. Maybe some information was inaccurate. If you can make something better, why wouldn't you?

When Mike Breaux was on our staff in Las Vegas and we were preparing to launch a new church there, we spent about seven months sharing the preaching load. He'd preach a weekend, and I'd preach a weekend. He'd do a midweek, and I'd do a midweek. I think both of us would say that we grew more as communicators during that era than during any other time in our lives because we were constantly giving each other critique and feedback. It was just so helpful.

DAVE: You've been preaching for twenty-plus years. How has your style changed through the years?

GENE: I'd say it took me nearly fifteen years to find my own voice in preaching. There's a period of time when you're so influenced by your mentors and other communicators that even without realizing it, you're subtly adopting their mannerisms and style. But then a time comes when you really find who you are and what your voice is, what your style is, what your comfort level is. And maybe even in the last five or six years, I think I've found my own voice and my own comfort level. Rather than asking, "Is this how Bob Russell would say it?" or "Is this how Bill Hybels or Charles Colson would say it?" now I say, "Is this how Gene Appel would say it?"

DAVE: What do you find fulfilling about communicating God's Word?

GENE: There is nothing like seeing the gospel come into contact with another human life and effect real change. You know no psychologist, no educator could ever effect that kind of change; only the work of God in the human heart can do it.

I remember one time after a service in Las Vegas, a young man—probably about twenty-seven years old—came up to me after the service and handed me a .38 bullet. I wasn't sure how to respond to that because nobody had ever handed me a bullet after a sermon.

"There is nothing like seeing the gospel come into contact with another human life and effect real change."

He said, "Here, Gene, I want you to have this."

And I asked, "What's this about?"

He said, "I was going to put that in my head this week, but you gave me a reason not to. What happened here today was just incredible, and I think maybe…maybe there is hope for me. Maybe there is a God that really cares and loves me."

I keep that bullet in the top drawer of my desk to this day, and it's a reminder of the power of this message. Now, I didn't do anything in this young man's life. God did. That's a humbling thing. You just think, "Man, I hope I steward this well because I don't want to do it any dishonor or damage. I want to be fully available to be the vessel God can use. I want to give him all the credit for everything that gets done because he's the one."

Can you see why I chose Gene Appel as the Relevant Illustrator? He wants to connect with his culture. You can't help but picture his examples scrolling through your mind. The reason those illustrations are vivid, even days later, is because they're relevant. Gene connects with this culture because he works at it and spends the necessary time in preparation.

Advice on Refining This Style
◆ *Establish the purpose of the message first.*
The featured communicator for the Practical Applicator chapter, Bob Russell, offers a caution to the Relevant Illustrator: "Most illustrations bubble up from applications. I don't begin

a sermon focusing on illustrations but rather ask, 'How is this going to apply to people's lives?' If I go to illustrations too quickly, I start building a sermon around the story. You don't build a building around a window. The window is strategically placed to let light in. But at times I'm tempted to use a great story and want to build an entire sermon around *it*." (See the "Happy" story on pages 93-94 and feel my pain.) Be relevant, but don't force the fit.

◆ *Consider the message from the listener's viewpoint.*
Sometimes it helps to picture who is out there listening to your diatribe and what they're going through personally. If you can make wise selections on which stories to include based on your listeners' needs and experiences, your illustrations can build a bridge instead of a barrier.

◆ *Springboard off current events.*
Relevancy is the ongoing, demanding challenge to produce fresh bread week after week. If you work to be relevant, you'll notice that listeners walk away shocked that something you said in a Bible study or sermon actually ties in with what they're experiencing in the community or their own lives.

One way to ensure such relevancy is to take advantage of what's being talked about in the news. For example, this is how I concluded a message:

Many of you enjoy watching the cable television show called *Trading Spaces*. More than twenty-eight million Americans watch it each week. For the show, neighbors trade homes for forty-eight hours and overhaul a room in a major way. Two weeks ago, the *Trading Spaces* celebrities pulled into Louisville.

This past week they were in our neighborhood, and to say that grown adults went crazy would be an understatement. The cul-de-sac was packed with groupies and curiosity seekers. Children and adults just stood around in hopes of a picture, an autograph, or a brief conversation with one of the designers.

The big hit was Ty. (What are you ladies smiling about?) Ty is a good-looking carpenter who has chiseled arms that are more muscular than mine. (No, I'm serious.) Women would never watch their husbands build a doghouse in the back yard, but they came from near and far just to watch Ty saw a two-by-four in half.

I asked my daughters, "What's the big deal? Just bring me a hammer and ask dear old dad to put on a tank top…" (That was their response too.)

Trading Spaces has captured the attention and viewership of homeowners around the country. Apparently the idea of trading spaces for forty-eight hours is quite appealing. But the idea isn't original to the Learning Channel.

Two thousand years ago, another carpenter traded spaces with you for six hours one Friday. He went to a cross as a perfect sacrifice; he took on all of your sins and mine so that you would never have to see a place called hell.

The congregation wasn't really expecting the spiritual application. When I said the words "Two thousand years ago, another carpenter traded spaces with you," the congregation's mood instantly changed. That phrase—"traded spaces with you"—further brought home the application. The listeners quickly surmised that the novelty of having celebrities in town paled to the relevancy of having their sins forgiven by a Jewish carpenter who was and is God in the flesh. The impact was possible because the illustration—borrowed from overwhelming media coverage—was a shared experience among congregation members.

◆ *Choose biblical illustrations whenever possible.*
If I have a choice between using a Bible story or a generic illustration, I'll almost always choose the Bible. This conditions people to go to the Bible for answers to today's problems. Perhaps the best reason this works is the promise in Isaiah 55:11 that "it will not return empty."

Since the Bible is the Word of God, the stories are easily relevant to your congregation or class. God in his infinite wisdom made certain that what was included relates to how you live your life right now. Being relevant goes beyond simply understanding your lesson material; it also includes an understanding of the setting. You must build a bridge from the setting in which the words were written to the contemporary society in which you preach or teach. Your lessons and messages must answer the spiritual questions in the lives of your listeners. If your communication scratches where they itch, then they'll return for more.

Your lessons and messages must answer the spiritual questions in the lives of your listeners.

For example, in John 15:5 Jesus talks about the importance of being rooted in the vine. Since people in that time period were familiar with growing grapes, they understood Jesus' relevant example. The modern-day equivalent may be plugging your cell phone battery into your car adapter in order to draw the power to recharge the battery.

◆ *Use old stories that are still relevant to today's world.*

Maybe you've heard the story about a preacher whose nagging wife died. As they carried her coffin to the grave, the pallbearers stumbled over a rock and dropped the casket. It burst open, and the jolt awoke the woman. She'd only been in a coma. She regained her health and lived for another two years. When she died, the pallbearers carried the casket along that same path. The husband pointed down and said, "Watch out for that rock."

While it may be an old joke, the dynamics at play in the story are still relevant to what husbands and wives face today.

◆ *Use caution with personal illustrations.*

In my opinion, personal illustrations are second only to biblical illustrations in their effectiveness. But personal illustrations are similar to salt—a little helps, and a lot ruins. Every once in a while, review your last few messages to make certain you aren't talking about yourself or your family more than you should. Also be certain that you rarely are the hero. People resonate more with your blunders than your triumphs. Plus, your victories can sound rather self-serving when shared from the lectern.

♦ *Incorporate relevant lists in addition to illustrations.*
Formulating and sharing lists can be of great value. Preparing them can be time-consuming, but they can invite different audience members into your talk with just a phrase or sentence. Through a relevant list, each listener can relate to one or two of your examples. For example, this is the list I used when talking about how the Christian life is filled with tests of humble obedience:

Personal illustrations are similar to salt—a little helps, and a lot ruins.

1. God says to bring the whole tithe into the storehouse. Do you say, "The church is always trying to pressure me for money"? Or would you respond with humble obedience and say, "Everything I have belongs to the Lord, and I need to give back"?

2. The Bible says, "Repent and be baptized." What's your response: "No, not me. I'm not going to be dunked"? Or would you ask, "What would God have me do?"

3. Wives should be submissive to their husbands. Do you respond with "No man is going to tell me what to do" or "Lord, help me to walk in your will, even if my instincts rebel"?

4. Husbands should love their wives as Christ loved the church. Do you respond with "I'm not romantic; that's just not me" or "Lord, help me demonstrate love and compassion so my wife feels cherished, needed, and appreciated"?

Balance the list so it's relevant to people. Would the list above be as good if I'd stopped after saying, "Wives, be submissive to your husbands"? Of course not! (It could also be dangerous to your health!) I would have alienated a good portion of my audience. When I speak about the husband's responsibility, I've balanced the list.

♦ *Use a "litmus test" for your illustrations.*
With each illustration, ask yourself some tough questions: Does this story tie in with the central theme of the talk? Is it pertinent to people's situations? Is it the correct length? Does it fit well in this message? If the answer to any of those questions is "no," save the illustration for another day.

◆ *Create powerful transitions.*

As is true with creative storytelling, relevant illustrating requires special attention to transitions. If you haven't attended to the entrance to and exit from an illustration, it loses its punch. Relevance helps, but it doesn't ensure success. Let me illustrate.

> I've heard a story about a person who witnessed a unique occurrence at a Special Olympics race. Seven handicapped kids lined up for the hundred-yard dash. The race started, and their arms and legs were pumping every which way. The crowd was cheering enthusiastically. Then the guy who was in first place tripped and fell to the ground. An amazing thing happened. One or two of the other runners stopped, walked back, picked up the fallen runner, and then finished the race together.[4]
>
> And some people say, "They're not as smart as we are."

If you're preaching on unity or compassion or reaching out to other people, you've got a good story. It's probably a "seven." But if you add that last line—"And some people say they're not as smart as we are"—you bring it home. Why? Because everybody has a relative or a friend or knows someone who is in a similar situation. The illustration becomes personal. It becomes relevant.

◆ *Keep it short.*

The best way to maximize the impact of your message is by meticulously weed-eating four-minute stories down to two and a half minutes. In so doing, you relieve the pressure of holding people's attention throughout a long story. Also, listeners will connect more easily with the relevance of the lesson if your illustration includes only the essential details rather than irrelevant facts.

Spend your last hours of preparation cutting and editing, fine-tuning so the cream rises to the top. Save your leftovers for another day when you find the right fit.

You may say, "But I need to fill up a thirty-minute time slot!" If that's your response, you need to change your perspective. You're not going into a pulpit or classroom to take up time. You are there as a mouthpiece for the King of kings and attempting to share God's message. Besides, if you normally go thirty minutes and occasionally go only twenty-five, don't expect to hear complaints from members who feel cheated! Quality beats quantity.

ENDNOTES

1 Michael Duduit, ed., *Communicate With Power: Insights From America's Top Communicators* (Grand Rapids, MI: Baker Books, a division of Baker Book House Company, 1996), 17.

2 Clyde E. Fant Jr. and William M. Pinson Jr., *20 Centuries of Great Preaching: An Encyclopedia of Preaching, Volume One: Biblical Sermons to Savonarola* (Waco, TX: Word Books Publisher, 1971), preface.

3 Duduit, ed., *Communicate With Power: Insights From America's Top Communicators*, 41.

4 Barbara Mikkelson, "Human(e) Race" (available online at www.snopes.com/glurge/special.htm), accessed January 6, 2004.

CHAPTER **12**

The Cultural Prophet

"Rather than cursing the darkness, we need to be lighting a candle."
—**Chuck Colson**

"If the trumpet does not sound a clear call, who will get ready for battle?" —**1 Corinthians 14:8**

The Cultural Prophet speaks to help people *confront* something.
The target is the listener's *conscience*.
Think Chuck Colson.

Similar styles: Revolutionary Leader, Direct Spokesman, Inspiring Orator

Words that describe this style: Single-minded, unintimidated, politically savvy, bold, visionary

You might be a Cultural Prophet if...

- you stay up-to-date on current trends and are "in the know" when it comes to society.
- you're glad to be the *example* and not the *exception* in order to blaze a trail for others to follow.
- your office has a few stacks of the Wall Street Journal, New York Times, and USA Today.
- you truly believe you can help reverse the downward spiral of our culture.
- you're consumed with taking a stand and influencing others to partner with you.
- you'd be willing to make an enemy if you believed the truth could help that individual.

About This Style

My father used to tell a story about an especially cold stretch of winter during the Civil War. The Union forces asked a farmer for permission for their troops to camp on his property. They also asked if it was OK for them to use some of his fence for firewood so the troops would survive through the night.

If it weren't for the Cultural Prophets informing us of the moral slide, we gradually would be lulled to sleep by it.

The farmer said, "You may only take off the top rung of the fence and use it for firewood."

The next morning as the sun came up, it quickly became apparent that the fence was completely gone. Yet the soldiers had not disobeyed their orders. Each different watch of soldiers had done as they were told. They had simply taken the top rung of the fence and used it for firewood.

Cultural Prophets are consumed with protecting the fence. They're wise enough to realize what happens over time when everyone takes off the top rung. They can't idly sit by and watch fences that desperately need to stay up come down. If it weren't for the Cultural Prophets informing us of the moral slide, we gradually would be lulled to sleep by it. This is reminiscent of the frog that doesn't jump out of a pot of water as the temperature escalates one degree at a time and is finally boiled alive. Cultural Prophets want to turn the tide before it's too late.

Zig Ziglar, the featured Persuasive Motivator, has a burning desire to influence this culture. He considers himself a Cultural Prophet and shared some thoughts about this communication style: "A lot of the teachers who would like to teach right from wrong have their hands tied because we're in this 'everything is relative' mind-set which, of course, is pure baloney! I've never heard of a businessperson who would be willing to hire an accountant or a treasurer who admitted that he or she was only *relatively* honest. And when I get home, my wife never asks me whether I have been *relatively* faithful. Some things are right, and some things are wrong."[1]

As Zig indicates, Cultural Prophets are not swayed by popular opinion and sometimes stand alone because of that. Biblical truth provides the measuring rod for them, whereas moral relativists use a sliding scale to determine the basis for their opinions. It's natural for these communicators to blatantly and boldly warn listeners about cultural decline. While confrontational in style, they're not overbearing or rude; in fact, most are quite winsome. But while others fear rocking the boat, the Cultural Prophet jumps into the action.

Even when fighting societal battles that appear likely to end in their defeat, Cultural Prophets proceed with courage and clarity of purpose. They may not possess gifts of leadership as Revolutionary Leaders do, but both styles understand that retreat is not an option. Cultural Prophets don't lead as much as they confront the listeners' conscience, pushing them to make a decision.

These communicators have embraced a biblical worldview and yearn to convey it to those who don't share that perspective.

Cultural Prophets also tend to be more intellectual and devour anything that acquaints them with the signs of the times. They have an uncanny knowledge of the culture's trends and habits.

Like watchmen in Ezekiel 33, Cultural Prophets sound the trumpet, clearly expressing the truth that the height of our culture's revival will be determined by the depth of our repentance. These communicators have embraced a biblical worldview and yearn to convey it to those who don't share that perspective. Their lessons have a sense of urgency, as if they bear an incredible burden for lost people to be found and believers to be strengthened. I refer to these warriors as "heralds of hope."

These speakers and teachers can bring meaning and understanding to a variety of people since they speak to the culture. For example, when the tragedies of September 11, 2001, occurred, the media and school systems didn't seek comfort and answers from the American Civil Liberties Union. They camped on the doorsteps of the clergy for interviews and input. My preaching partner and I separately were on six different radio and television stations. People were longing for answers to questions like "Where is God when these tragedies strike?" It was a surreal experience three days later to be sitting in front of a microphone of the largest secular radio station in the state, being allowed to read a passage from the New Testament during the highest drive-time audience. In the midst of those tumultuous times, people who would never enter a church were listening in their cars to what the Bible says to our culture.

If this is not your natural style, to grow in it may require an increase in boldness. And like it or not, a time will come when our world and your church folks will desperately need to hear a bold message. Such a message will resonate with listeners who long to be challenged and motivated to stem the tide of moral decay. Although this style may seem foreign for you, using it could positively change the direction of a class, a congregation, or even a community. If you are a Cultural Prophet, you track the trends and help to head people in the right direction. Let me just say that you are needed.

Jesus, a Cultural Prophet

Jesus used this communication style in a variety of settings. For example, he challenged his listeners to "surpass the righteousness of the Pharisees." Talk about changing a culture! He couldn't have levied such an expectation if he wasn't familiar with the people and the culture he was there to reach. Consider the emotion Jesus showed when he overlooked the city of Jerusalem and cried out due to the residents' unwillingness to reach out to him (see Matthew 23:37). His messages rang with warnings laced with hope. Jesus was a prophet whose words confronted society when it was moving in the wrong direction.

Chuck Colson, a Cultural Prophet

If you are more than forty years old, you remember our featured Cultural Prophet as President Nixon's right-hand man. In a letter to this gentleman, Nixon wrote, "Your vision, energy, and drive are second to no one's."

How true. Prior to this man's conversion, his political clout was unparalleled. But when Chuck Colson came to Christ, his passion shifted; since that day he has not ceased to be a lighthouse for Christ in the midst of a spiritually darkened culture. He still has political clout, but it takes a back seat to his relationship with Jesus Christ.

Colson's intelligence and political savvy helped Nixon succeed. Colson was one of the most trusted advisors and, for the most part, was totally shielded from the knowledge of the Watergate scandal.

In a biography of Colson, John Perry gives us this insight as to why an innocent man like Colson would plead guilty to a crime that both his lawyer and judge were not even acquainted with. Perry explains, "He felt called as a Christian to do so…Colson didn't become a Christian because he went to prison; he went to prison because he became a Christian."[2]

It's impossible to be a Cultural Prophet if you answer only to those who rule the political kingdoms of this world. Chuck Colson has impacted tens of thousands because he is governed by the expectations of a spiritual kingdom. While he was in prison, God laid on Colson's heart a ministry to inmates. It's not glamorous, but it sure is necessary. Because of his commitment, Colson has had a hand in seeing thousands come to Christ.

If you are in the under-forty crowd, you know Chuck Colson as the chairman and founder of Prison Fellowship. You've probably heard him speak at a convention and appreciated his desire for our culture to turn to Christ.

Chuck Colson is able to communicate to people of varying backgrounds, social strata, and intellectual levels. He is one of the few people who feels at home talking one-on-one with a death row inmate or sitting in the Oval Office with the president. Since communication requires a connection between people, that ability is of paramount importance.

Interview With Chuck Colson

DAVE: How and when did you realize you had the gift of communication?

CHUCK: I always loved to speak, and a teacher challenged me to develop that gift. Also, my dad wanted me to be on the debate team. He would say that he would rather see me on the debate team than the high school football team. Through time I became a champion debater. After law school, I found that I loved the disputation. Later in life, I discovered the real joy in preaching—to be able to feel that exchange. If I don't sense that back-and-forth exchange with my audience, then I'm just talking.

DAVE: What are some of your goals when you're speaking?

CHUCK: Whether I'm speaking to ten thousand people or one-to-one, I watch their eyes. I'm not very good on television because I'm looking at a camera instead of a person. My goal is to engage the listeners individually, and that's why it helps me to watch their eyes.

My goal is to engage the listeners individually, and…it helps me to watch their eyes.

Notice how a black preacher will pause for the "amens." But if he pauses and doesn't get one, he'll say it as a question—"amen?" Then the people will say, "amen." That preacher is trying to create a dialogue instead of a monologue because a monologue is boring. If I look out and see by the looks on their faces that they're not engaged, then I may have to add a story to better explain my point or to engage them.

DAVE: What's the most rewarding aspect of preaching?

CHUCK: I want to engage the audience. I'm constantly asking myself, "Am I getting through?" The reward is to be able to get across a concept—the "aha" moment. Gratification comes when you've painted a word picture and the light comes on in the listener's mind. Their eyes say "aha," and you can see that they got it.

DAVE: Let's talk about how communication has changed for preachers.

CHUCK: It's a different world these days. Back in the eighteenth century when Jonathan Edwards preached "Sinners in the Hands of an Angry God," he preached from a word-for-word manuscript and never looked up. He just read it, and yet people were crying and clinging to the pillars within the church. Nowadays that message and method couldn't have the same impact or response because in this culture we're too visually driven. It would never work.

DAVE: Do you go through a preparation routine?

CHUCK: I just spoke to fifty congressmen last night on Capitol Hill. I wrote out on a legal pad about five pages of notes, then I condensed them to one sheet by listing just the key points. That sheet was tucked in my Bible. Typically I try to spend an hour alone with my notes. If I can get one hour—uninterrupted—before speaking, that's my security blanket. I may or may not look at those notes during the message. Last night they were sitting inside my Bible, and I looked at them once. If needed, I also have all the longer quotes written out for reference on a small piece of paper.

Remember, I'm watching their eyes to sense if they're not engaged or if I need to do a better job of explaining a point. In fact, last night I made major adjustments and added illustrations a couple of times.

DAVE: Who are you able to reach that others may not be able to reach?

CHUCK: I reach prisoners the best. I get the best response out of them. Give me my choice of a crowd to speak to, and it would be them. I love to go to prison—that way!

DAVE: What's the most intimidating group for you to address?

CHUCK: I immediately think of a recent speaking engagement. In May [of 2003] I was invited to address my alma mater at the Brown University Commencement Forum. Many of these schools have become bastions of liberalism. I put a great deal of work into it and chose to speak to that challenging crowd on ethics and integrity. I titled my talk "Can the Ivy League Teach Ethics?"

The basic premise of my talk was "no." The gentleman who introduced me was an associate professor of public policy. After I spoke he came to me and indicated that he was in complete agreement with everything I'd said.

With a crowd like that, you've got to be a little shrewd. By that I mean you don't stand there with your Bible and quote chapter and verse, but you use the biblical concepts to make the case for ethics. I firmly believe that prudence is a cardinal virtue; you must argue prudentially in language a hardened secular crowd can understand.

DAVE: What are some of the biggest challenges Christian communicators currently face?

CHUCK: One of the biggest challenges of preaching today is speaking effectively to the postmoderns. When a sermon speaks of absolute truth, you and I immediately think of the standard of

God's Word and the person of Jesus Christ. Postmoderns don't hear it that way. Their educational upbringing has caused a language barrier.

DAVE: What are some of your concerns about preachers these days?

CHUCK: I worry about some preachers who put themselves on the throne rather than Christ. They are the heroes of the story. What many don't realize is that they won't engage their audience that way. Self-deprecating humor wins people to you more so than being the hero. I talk in my book *Being the Body* of how some preachers seem to put themselves on a pedestal. They make themselves the focus of their preaching or writing. Transparency and self-deprecation show vulnerability, and yet I see a lot of preachers who aren't willing to do that. My advice would be "Don't let yourself get in the way of the communication!"

"Don't let yourself get in the way of the communication!"

DAVE: That's a great reminder for all who teach or preach.

CHUCK: Maybe you've heard about the four prisons we started through Prison Fellowship. The inmates there have Bible studies for some five hours a day. Typically 70 percent of inmates repeat their offenses within twelve months of their release. With the prisons we're running, the recidivism study that's about to come out after five years of research shows that only 8 percent from our prisons re-offended after they got out. It's unbelievable what the Word of God can do. We started the first prison outside of Sugarland, Texas, with the help of then-Governor George W. Bush. He hadn't been governor long enough to know what you're not supposed to do! So he gave us permission to start a Christian prison. They told him he was going to be sued. And George W. Bush said, "Go ahead and let 'em sue me." He's a very gutsy man.

So we started that prison six years ago. Recently the president invited us in to present to him the report of the University of Pennsylvania demonstrating that recidivism was only 8 percent. He invited us to bring in some graduates of the program. What a particular thrill that was for me to bring ex-offenders to the White House!

When the president walked into the Roosevelt Room for the meeting, he nodded to me, nodded to the attorney general and secretary of labor who were sitting around the table, walked right over to one of the African-American inmates, embraced him, and said, "I remember meeting you in Texas. You're a good man. Remember what the Scripture says about God using the foolish things of the world to shame the wise and the mighty." Then for the hour that followed, the inmates witnessed to the president, and we closed in prayer. It was like biblical times, seeing prisoners witness to the most powerful man in the world.

Now when I tell that story, the emphasis isn't on me. I'm not the one on the pedestal.

DAVE: So even though you met with the president, you are not the hero of the story. President Bush is the hero for his interest in the prisoners.

CHUCK: Not only that, but the prisoners are the heroes! They have the ear of the president. What a thrill that those convicts transformed by the gospel are witnessing to the president of the United States through their actions. What an inspiration that illustration can be to them and to others.

DAVE: What is a weakness of your style as a Cultural Prophet?

CHUCK: Sometimes I'll look out in the audience, and I'll see my wife, Patty. I'll see her shaking her head, and I realize that I've just used the term *deconstructionist*. The majority of the people have no idea what I'm talking about. My cultural terminology can get ahead of the crowd's understanding. So I need to do a better job of defining things, or the message doesn't come through.

DAVE: Can you think of an example?

CHUCK: Recently I was on a CCN broadcast, and people were asking questions beamed in by satellite. A thirteen-year-old girl asked a great question: "What exactly is moral truth? I don't quite understand what it means."

This is how I answered her:

Moral truth is the absolute standard that we point to in order to govern our behavior in virtually any area of life. It's what is right and what, over the ages, has been recognized as that which is true for all people of all time. The book *Mere Christianity* starts out on the proposition of the *Tao*, a Chinese term, meaning that there has been a truth that has been known through the ages. It's sometimes called natural law. It's a standard by which we govern our behavior. Every society throughout Western civilization has believed this; it's a moral code. In the postmodern age, everybody has their own formulation of what is real and what is not real. Everything is subjective. There is no truth. This is what Stanley Fish, the leading deconstructionist, argues on American life. This is the prevailing view on college campuses. You have to first do what Francis Schaeffer talked about—you have to first establish truth before you can present the truth.

"My cultural terminology can get ahead of the crowd's understanding."

Well, I finished fumbling through my confusing answer on moral truth. Beside me was David Neff, the editor of Christianity Today. David said to this thirteen-year-old girl, "When I was a teen, I got my first car—a Volkswagon Beetle. After some time, I had a problem with the oil. My dad gave me an owner's manual to study. There is an analogy here to moral truth: God has made us and has provided an owner's manual in the Bible, and that contains the standard of moral truth."

With that, the crowd broke into applause because his simple answer was clear and could be understood by this teen. I, the "great communicator," was unable to do that. I couldn't get that concept across to a thirteen-year-old girl because I was too hung up on my own, far-more-complicated understanding!

DAVE: You've studied this culture and its continued moral slide. What have you determined about our society and the next generation we're raising?

CHUCK: Just like Brown University, they have a different understanding of truth because ethics to them is "do what you want." Are you familiar with the Zogby Poll results concerning ethics in American colleges?[3] The findings that the National Association of Scholars released are frightening. A large majority of this year's college graduates reports that their professors tell them there are no clear and uniform standards of right and wrong. The Zogby

Poll revealed that although 97 percent of all seniors believe college has equipped them to perform ethically in their future professional lives, when asked which statement about ethics was most often transmitted by their professors, 73 percent selected the proposition "What is right and wrong depends on differences in individual values and cultural diversity." Only 25 percent picked "There are clear and uniform standards of right and wrong by which everyone should be judged."

So indeed the students truly thought they'd been taught ethics when in reality they were taught relativism.

DAVE: What do you see as the role of a prophet?

CHUCK: To try to see what God is saying and to speak to the church on his behalf, to challenge and critique and thereby to motivate people to live as God has commanded us to live, and in the process to call our culture to moral accountability.

DAVE: You and I agree that of the communication styles covered in this book, the term *Cultural Prophet* is an accurate description of how God has chosen to use you. What Old Testament prophet are you most similar to?

CHUCK: I've never really thought about that. I would suspect Jeremiah would be the person. He always gave people hope and promise. When I was in prison, there were times that I wrestled with discouragement. My good friend Father John Neuhaus says, "Despair is a sin; it denies the sovereignty of God."

I never get over the paradox of the gospel. God's done more than I ever imagined. My life is the greatest living example of providence.

Before leaving Chuck's office, I awkwardly asked his assistant to take a picture of Chuck and me. She willingly obliged. I'm glad to have a visual reminder of the interview. But when my pictures came back, I noticed a plaque on the wall in the background. It contained a quote from Father John Neuhaus. The words were as clear in the photograph as the message they conveyed: "Undaunted we are enlisted for the duration, bearing witness to the truth." Those words sum up the battle cry of the Cultural Prophet.

Chuck's communication skills and power of persuasion were obvious early in his career. Biographer John Perry described the Chuck Colson of the 1960s like this: "Colson...laced his speeches with observations and pronouncements on political trends of the moment."[4] Sounds like a pretty good description of a Cultural Prophet. Chuck Colson faithfully communicates God's truth to a spiritually sagging society. We need more "heralds of hope" like him.

Advice on Refining This Style

◆ *Change the culture from the inside.*

I love Rick Rusaw and Eric Swanson's new book *The Externally Focused Church*. In it, the authors describe how the Cultural Prophet can spark societal changes by getting involved: "Society is like a stream. If we don't like the direction it's going, we face a choice: We can either stand on the banks, yelling and screaming about what is wrong with the stream, or we can roll up our pant legs and wade in."[5] Cultural Prophets aren't afraid to get wet. They may dive into the parent-teacher association of the school system, a political campaign, or local sports program. Intuitively they realize the way to make a difference is by getting involved and thus earning the right to be heard.

Cultural prophets aren't afraid to get wet.

◆ *Do your homework.*

Cultural Prophets study well. They do their homework. They know the society and the trends of culture because they've invested time in studying. They can sense when we're on the verge of collapse or renewal. They thrive on putting their study and research to good use by communicating what they've learned to the rest of us who are "culturally challenged." To improve your cultural finesse, do as Cultural Prophets do: Watch the news, read the paper, and engage in conversations with people who are different from you.

◆ *Sound the church bell instead of a fire alarm.*

David Enyart writes, "In Greek mythology, Odysseus and his crew sail near the dangerous 'island of sirens' and the seductive music woos them to the shore. To shut out the tempting strains, Odysseus stuffs the ears of his sailors with cotton. Later, Orpheus and his seamen sail by the same enticing island. Orpheus protects his crew in a different manner: He takes out his lyre and *plays sweeter music* than that which wafts from the island."[6]

Christianity needn't be known as a religion of "don'ts."

The strong choleric approach doesn't reap that big of a harvest. *Telling* people the way is different from *showing* them the way and stressing the benefits. I'm not suggesting that you neglect mentioning the disciplines and consequences of following Christ. I'm saying that Christianity needn't be known as a religion of "don'ts." Jesus said, "All men will know that you are my disciples, if you love one another" (John 13:35). Sure sounds like a "do" to me. No blaring fire alarm—simply an invitation to a countercultural lifestyle that's accompanied by some pretty cool eternal rewards. The most effective Cultural Prophets enjoy stressing the positives that can result from a culture committed to Christ.

◆ *Avoid the "Pet Peeve of the Month" approach.*

It may be easy to choose what you want to gripe about and harp on it incessantly. But your lessons should be based on facts and trends rather than on your social pet peeve of the month. Hopping from issue to issue, developing cases for each choice concern, diminishes the power of your communication. Be honest about the things that are improving in society, and consistently convey the vision for a countercultural kingdom.

◆ *Make Christ—not yourself—the focus.*

Preachers and teachers need to stay off the pedestal. This caution, which Chuck pointed out, is true for every style. But because of their zeal for influencing society, Cultural Prophets can seem larger than life to their listeners. If you're not careful, the audience may

remember you more than your message. When that occurs, your
efforts at communicating have failed. The Apostle Paul says in
2 Corinthians 4:5, "For we do not preach ourselves, but Jesus
Christ as Lord, and ourselves as your servants for Jesus' sake."

Max Lucado frequently will begin his sermons with a prayer
that closes with these words: "Now we receive your teaching, O
Father. Please have mercy on the one who speaks—his sins are
many. May we see Jesus today and just him."

Such an attitude goes a long way in impacting your listeners by
aiming their allegiance to Christ.

◆ *Take a stand—at the appropriate time.*
Rick Atchley, who preaches in Fort Worth, Texas, helped me to
understand what it means to be a prophet. Allow me to paraphrase what I learned from him:

> Throughout the life of the leader there is an ongoing tension. It
> pulls us between being seen as the priest who lovingly ministers
> to the flock, and acting as the prophet who boldly challenges
> them. This reality demands that a transition take place in virtu-
> ally every ministry. Over the course of time in any growing
> organization, the leader typically moves from being a priest to
> being a prophet. The problem is that there are a lot of preachers
> who *start out trying to be a prophet* and telling people what to do.
> But it's often too early for that. These preachers haven't earned
> the right to be heard. Respect and credibility are the result of
> years of being a loving pastor and priest to the people. Only
> through years of faithful ministry does one earn the right to be
> heard as a prophet.
>
> Other pastors have served faithfully for years in a priestly role,
> but now their congregations are looking for prophetic leader-
> ship, longing to be challenged. These preachers, however, are
> content to remain 'crouched' in the security of their priestly
> positions rather than standing up to be the prophets God has
> called them to be.[7]

Paul said to the church at Ephesus, "Therefore put on the full
armor of God, so that when the day of evil comes, you may be

able to stand your ground, and after you have done everything, to stand" (Ephesians 6:13).

ENDNOTES

1 Said in an interview by Zig Ziglar to David Yoho Jr. on a CD titled A *View from the Top: Featuring Zig Ziglar, CPAE*, produced by the National Speakers Association, 2003.

2 John Perry, *Charles Colson: A Story of Power, Corruption, and Redemption* (Nashville, TN: Broadman & Holman Publishers, 2003), x.

3 Author's note: The National Association of Scholars is America's foremost higher education reform group. Located in Princeton, it has forty-six state affiliates and more than four thousand professors, graduate students, administrators, and trustees as members. These results were released in July 2002.

4 Perry, *Charles Colson: A Story of Power, Corruption, and Redemption*, 30.

5 Rick Rusaw and Eric Swanson, *The Externally Focused Church* (Loveland, CO: Group Publishing, Inc., 2004).

6 David A. Enyart, *Creative Anticipation: Narrative Sermon Designs for Telling the Story* (Philadelphia, PA: Xlibris Corporation, 2002), 9.

7 Dave Stone, *Keeping Your Head Above Water* (Loveland, CO: Group Publishing, Inc., 2002), 37.

CHAPTER **13**

The Unorthodox Artist

"People get bored with seeing and hearing the same old thing week after week. When they know what's coming, they tune it out; the higher the predictability, the lower the communication. Constant change gives a look of freshness and keeps people interested."
—**Andy Stanley and Ed Young**[1]

"They brought the donkey and the colt, placed their cloaks on them, and Jesus sat on them. A very large crowd spread their cloaks on the road, while others cut branches from the trees and spread them on the road. The crowds that went ahead of him and those that followed shouted,
'Hosanna to the Son of David!'
'Blessed is he who comes in the name of the Lord!'
'Hosanna in the highest!'
When Jesus entered Jerusalem, the whole city was stirred and asked, 'Who is this?'
The crowds answered, 'This is Jesus, the prophet from Nazareth in Galilee.'"
—**Matthew 21:7-11**

The Unorthodox Artist speaks to help people *experience* something.
The target is the listener's *senses*.
Think Rob Bell.

Similar styles: Creative Storyteller, Passionate Teacher, Inspiring Orator

Words that describe this style: Unconventional, artistic, risky, creative, nonconforming, unique, free-spirited, imaginative, surprising

You might be an Unorthodox Artist if...

- you usually prefer the out-of-the-ordinary approach instead of the typical.
- you're apt to spend more of your own money on an important prop for your sermon than you did for your spouse's birthday and Christmas gifts combined.
- you're a *Seinfeld* fan who relates to Kramer more than George.
- you get a thrill whenever you shock your audience.
- you thank somebody who calls you "bizarre."
- your church is more surprised when they see a pulpit on the stage than when they see a goat.
- you salivate when a critic says, "Well, we've never done it that way before."

About This Style

In the 1980s, Mike Breaux—now of Willow Creek Community Church—was the youth minister at a historic church in the heart of downtown Lexington, Kentucky. It was his turn to preach on a Sunday night.

Most members remember his sermon that evening. As often is the case with downtown churches, the church occasionally attracted some "strays" when the front doors were unlocked. On this particular evening, a smelly homeless man wearing rags, a hat, old clothes, and a ratty coat came into the sanctuary. Members who crossed paths with him looked the other way. The row he chose to sit in experienced a sudden emptiness as other pew warmers made a hasty exodus. No one spoke to him. It was as if people thought, "If we ignore him, maybe he'll go away."

When the song service ended and the special music was over, it was time for the sermon. But there was no Mike. Everyone looked around for him. Some were worried that something had happened to him because Mike wouldn't miss an opportunity to preach. Awkwardness reigned for a couple of uncomfortable minutes until finally the "homeless man" stood up and began shuffling in the direction of the pulpit. As he did, he began to shed his disguise one layer at a time. In a matter of seconds, sur-prised members began to recognize the man they had ostracized as their very own youth minister. His opening line was "Turn in your Bibles to James, chapter 2, as tonight we're going to talk about favoritism."

As you read about the Unorthodox Artist, you'll probably think of a person who fits the description. She enjoys pushing the envelope. He thrives on stretching himself and thinking outside the box. These communicators are highly creative and could be characterized as renegades. If the Scholarly Analytic is characterized as mild sauce, then the Unorthodox Artist is hot sauce with a couple of extra jalapeños.

These communicators make memories that last a lifetime for church members.

Unorthodox Artists may be drawn to the arts, and they'll use anything they can think of—drama, dance, movie clips, sculpture, humor, mime, painting, smells, sound, video, and more—to try to reach a variety of people. These communi-cators make memories that last a lifetime for church members. Listeners may never again be able to see a prop used during a message without thinking of that message.

Catching an audience off-guard is one of the Unorthodox Artists' greatest joys, as they thrive on the element of surprise. They may not resort to shouting, but they'll do whatever it takes to capture the audience's attention and drive home the point of the lesson.

This may surprise you, but I've found Unorthodox Artists to be some of the most well-prepared and diligent communicators. The size of the audience doesn't concern them. Whether preparing a lesson for a few or for thousands, Unorthodox Artists are con-sumed with everything flowing perfectly. In contrast, Engaging Humorists have a little more of a tendency to wing it.

Many popular speakers utilize this style to keep their audience coming back so as not to miss anything. Andy Stanley of North Point Community Church in Alpharetta, Georgia, handed out money to every church member during a sermon in order to see how God could multiply their efforts. Senior Pastor Ed Young drove a Mercedes onto the platform at Fellowship Church in Grapevine, Texas, and preached from it for two weeks. Kyle Idleman, who is on our preaching team here at Southeast, covered the platform with street signs and worked through his message by discussing the meaning of each one. Bob Russell, our senior minister, walked us through the meaning of the Passover meal a week before Easter with close-ups of food items that the whole congregation could see.

Rick Rusaw, who preaches at LifeBridge Christian Church in Longmont, Colorado, set up crosses at various stations throughout the sanctuary. During the service, he asked the congregation to go to the stations. While music played and the people prayed, members nailed to the cross paper lists of their sins. The sporadic echo of nails pounding throughout the sanctuary was extremely moving.

Our featured communicator for this style once shaved a guy's head while preaching on the Nazarite vow. On another occasion, he explained the Day of Atonement with three props: a man dressed up as the high priest, a chair, and a goat. He set the goat free to leave the building, which allowed him to repeatedly drive home the forgiveness we have through Jesus Christ with the phrase "The goat has left the building." On the audio CD, you'll hear him start his sermon by putting together all of the ingredients for salsa and making it in a blender.

I used to do more unorthodox artistry because I saw its value and enjoyed it. But since it requires more creative-thinking time, planning, and preparation, it gave way to the routine of more "normal" sermons. But there is a huge value when you make the effort to add variety to sermons.

Thanks to the challenges and prodding of a friend on staff, I've returned to the discipline of forcing myself out of the box. I've made it a goal to do at least two visual sermons each year. It gives our people a break, and it allows them to learn from an uncharacteristic style. So I've done monologues of Bible characters, memorized a children's book, and preached on parenting by moving room to room in a makeshift home built onstage. Recently I even crafted an entire message around a series of movie clips as I taught from a theater seat on the stage.

If you're a nonconformist, then you'll find hope and encouragement by reading this chapter. Or you may be like me in that, over time, your preaching style has become safer and more conservative. If so, it will be healthy for you to read this chapter more than once! For those of you who are creatively challenged—perhaps even set in your ways—I hope these pages will move you out of your comfort zone and breathe even more life into your ministry. Remember, regardless of your natural way of communicating, every Christian leader will have to venture into each of these thirteen styles at various points. The variety of ministry settings and circumstances demand it. David Enyart writes this warning: "Frequently, creativity and imaginativeness are casualties of ministerial education. Ministers start to mistrust or ignore their own creative impulses; they come to view imagination as a child's *play toy* rather than *an essential tool* for vibrant communication."[2]

> When I get out of my comfort zone, my preaching improves because I rely on the Lord more. His power is made perfect in my weakness.

Besides, when I get out of my comfort zone, my preaching improves because I rely on the Lord more. His power is made perfect in my weakness (2 Corinthians 12:10).

Jesus, an Unorthodox Artist

Jesus was an Unorthodox Artist at times. He showed signs of unconventionality throughout his earthly ministry. Consider this:

• Is it normal for a twelve-year-old to hold court with the religious leaders in the temple and draw a crowd? (See Luke 2:41-49.)

• Is it typical to take spittle and mix it with dirt and place it on someone's eyes when you could just touch him so he could see clearly? (See Matthew 9:29-30; Matthew 20:34; and Mark 8:23-24.)

• Is it common behavior for a Jewish man to have a conversation with a Samaritan woman and pave the way for many to believe? (See John 4:7-26.)

• Is it wise for a man at the height of his popularity to turn up the heat with a radical message of hating father, mother, brother, and sister in an effort to thin out the uncommitted? (See Luke 12:52-53.)

• Is it kosher for a peasant carpenter to single-handedly shout an impromptu speech, turn some tables over, and close down a lucrative but dishonest business in the temple? (See Mark 11:15-17.)

Now, I don't suggest trying *all* those things in your Sunday school class next week. You have to admit that Jesus was unorthodox.

Rob Bell, an Unorthodox Artist

The under-thirty crowd especially seems to enjoy employing this technique. Our featured Unorthodox Artist, Rob Bell from Grandville, Michigan, is one example. Rob epitomizes this style. His friends and family describe his communication approach as random, visual, eclectic, unique, and always honest and biblical. The entire first year of Mars Hill Bible Church, Rob preached on the book of Leviticus—and the church grew from zero to three thousand members. (Talk about being seeker-sensitive! Maybe you've been preaching on the wrong topics or text.) In just five years of existence, his church has grown in attendance to nearly ten thousand.

Rob explained his thought process in a Leadership magazine article:

I knew opening with Leviticus—foreign words to today's culture—was risky. But the bigger the risk, the more need for the Spirit and the more glory for God to get...

Each week when I invite people to open their Bibles, they cheer! When I say, "Please turn with me to chapter..." the congregation will erupt, "Five!" and a flurry of page turning begins. It's become a tradition...

My generation thinks and converses visually. Film is the dominant language of our culture. We relate with images and pictures and metaphors. Leviticus is perfect for us. It's one image after another. Blood, animals, and clothing of certain colors—provocative pictures a person can ponder forever...

A year after beginning, the series on Leviticus came to an end, and it was time to move on.

Now I'm preaching Numbers.[3]

Rob is a summer favorite at Willow Creek Community Church. He's been a main speaker at the National Pastors Convention. He is the Robin Williams of evangelical ministers.

Interview With Rob Bell

DAVE: At the time of this interview, you are thirty-two years old. When did you first sense that you had a gift in the area of communication?

ROB: When I was in college, some friends and I started a punk rock band. We started playing gigs. I was the lead singer. I couldn't sing, but I was the singer. However, writing lyrics and putting on these shows tapped into something deep. I thought, "Whatever this is, I want to do this with my life." The summer after college, the band kind of fell apart, and I knew that I was supposed to go to seminary. That's all I knew. So at the age of twenty-one, I volunteered to preach my first sermon (I don't know what possessed me!). I got up to preach, and I took off my sandals because I knew I was on holy ground. God, at that moment, seemed to say to me, "If you teach this book, I will take care of everything else."

That experience changed my life. In my mind, I reasoned that all of my angst and rebellion and subversive tendencies and nonconforming could be channeled into something which was beautiful, creative, and good for God.

> "I got up to preach, and I took off my sandals because I knew I was on holy ground."

DAVE: Who has influenced your communication style?

ROB: David Letterman, Bono, Beck. Beck's music is nice because he begs, borrows, and steals from any genre—rap, disco, whatever. It's interesting that we're talking about communication style because I'd be like the guy who collects everybody else's junk. I, too, will beg, borrow, and steal from any style or genre.

DAVE: So if it can touch you, it can touch somebody else. That's why you are the Unorthodox Artist.

ROB: I suppose so. I vary my methods. I might be straight expositional one week—here's Greek word number one, here's Greek word number two, here are four other texts where this word is used, here are three insights and two central questions we need to ask ourselves in regard to application. Then the following week I might have a goat up there with me. The next week, I might center around one image, a picture built around one line or one verse and one possible interpretation of one Hebrew word.

I'm preparing a series on the Ten Commandments right now, and I'm all over the place. Generally there's a visual element. Sometimes I preach very slowly and sometimes very quickly. Sometimes I don't speak. Sometimes I've preached silent sermons where the whole sermon was on the screen and I just stood there.

"I'll try any method to get you thinking, feeling, touching, and smelling. I want to assault as many senses as possible."

DAVE: You are often described as being very visual when you teach or preach, using props, visuals, and so on.

ROB: I bought ten thousand pieces of modeling clay one time. Each person received his or her own chunk of modeling clay because we are God's workmanship—we are God's artwork. So the whole time, you're holding your piece of clay. I'll try any method to get you thinking, feeling, touching, and smelling. I want to assault as many senses as possible. I want as many contact points as possible. So I'll be doing something with a prop, then I'll read a text, then I'll go back to the prop, then I'll tell a story, now back to the text, now back to the screen. I want to work off of many different surfaces.

DAVE: How did Jesus use different teaching methods?

ROB: I think of the story where Jesus curses a fig tree, which was a symbol of leadership—specifically spiritual leadership. Nobody talked against the sages back then. So instead of saying to the disciples, "All the religious leaders are corrupt. The whole place has gone to hell," Jesus simply curses the fig tree as he goes up the hill and moves on. If you're a disciple, you're thinking, "Oh! He's saying something about the temple." Brilliant. Just brilliant teaching.

DAVE: Your family and friends say you approach preaching as an artist would. There are no definitions or boundaries. It is whole-person communication. Is that an accurate description?

ROB: Well, I have no sense of any rules. Seminary students or other pastors may say you have to have an introduction. Why?

Sometimes I purposefully want people totally in the dark. Sometimes I even want you in the dark for forty-five minutes. I want you to be thinking, "Where is he going with this?" Because if you're asking that question, I've got you.

DAVE: Does everyone bring Bibles?

ROB: We hand them to people as they come in. The page numbers are always up on the screen. We never assume that people have ever opened a Bible. I'm obsessed with how to say things so that you'd be able to track at least to some degree even if you didn't know anything beforehand. When I hear preachers say something like "We were really blessed by sanctification," I wince. I'm thinking, "Oh, bummer." Or they'll say, "You all know this song. Let's join in the chorus." And I'm thinking, "Shun the pagan." Or they'll say, "You all know the disciple John." And I'm thinking, "Well, nobody here *knows* the disciple John." So instead I might say, "These words were written by this guy named Paul; he was a Jewish rabbi."

> "We never assume that people have ever opened a Bible."

DAVE: What are some ways you make the imagery of Scriptures come alive in your preaching?

ROB: I did a series on Song of Songs and explained how the different mention of plants had sexual overtones. So I had a guy who owns Fruitbasket Flowerland come and fill the stage with plants from all over the world that are mentioned in Song of Songs. Then for my message, I walked through the sexual images of those particular plants found in God's Word. That was so awesome.

DAVE: What's the biggest challenge you have to overcome because of your natural style?

ROB: Every teaching for me has to have an arc. Very few preachers understand arc. Underneath it all, there is always a line. We're going somewhere. There is going to be a moment. Until you have an arc, you have no story. Screenwriters are masters of this. There has to be a story—no matter what it is. Otherwise, it's three observations about something and a conclusion.

This is the difference between a newscast and a movie. A newscast is a series of linear fragments that are lined up with no relation to each other, and you can turn it off at any point because of that. But why is it that in a high school American history class a teacher will show a three-minute clip of the movie *The Patriot*, and every kid who is usually dialed out and bored out of their minds is riveted to that three-minute segment? When, all of a sudden, the screen goes blue and says "video stop," the whole class goes "ahhh..." How can you be sucked in completely in three minutes? The answer: Because there's an arc. It's going somewhere. So until I find the arc, there isn't much happening in my preparation.

DAVE: Give me an example of an arc.

ROB: I'm preaching on the Ten Commandments in a couple of weeks. I'm speaking on the commandment "Do not lie." So of course I'm going to hang planets and build a solar system in our worship center! In the middle, in between the screens, I'm going to have a sun lowered down on a pulley. Because on the first day of Creation, God said, "Let there be light." Yet God didn't create the sun, moon, or stars until the fourth day. That means light exists independently of the celestial bodies. We generally think of "light" as the sun, but "light" is something that exists independent of the movement of the planets. So the Scriptures say that God is light, that light isn't something that comes from the planets but is something that is central to the core characteristics of God. So when I lie, I'm creating darkness. I'm concealing the very nature of how things are. That's the reason lies are exhausting. When you lie, you're trying to figure out which lie you told and how to retell it.

For me the arc is the question, "How many of you today are in darkness in some way? You have set yourself up against the very nature of one of the core attributes of the universe. And it's exhausting because you're actually creating darkness." So I'm going to turn off all the lights, and I'm going to have spotlights come on. The seats will be in darkness, but there will be this big light in the middle of the room. And I'm simply going to ask, "Do you need to get up out of your seat right now? Do you need to get up and physically, as a public act, step from dark into light?"

So to answer your original question, the weakness of this style is that until I have an arc, I'm just talking.

FRIENDS AND FAMILY INTERRUPT: I'll tell you what the downside of this style is. He can't do it unless it's a masterpiece. Rob is like an artist. He has to be excited or proud or feel good about the art he's presenting. If he doesn't, it eats him up inside. It's tough to sustain that for too many weeks in a row.

ROB: I don't do well forty-eight Sundays in a local church! That is the downside. I don't do well week after week after week after week because I don't think it's good for our congregation. If we don't blow the roof off, I'm miserable.

DAVE: What discipline has been most beneficial to your preaching and teaching?

ROB: I've discovered that there has to be a massive input of new ideas. I'll read anything, any idea from anywhere. I devour books. I'm obsessed. I inhale ideas from all and take them captive. Many of the books I read are not Christian, because I see God's truth in other voices.[4]

DAVE: What changes have you made in your speaking since attending seminary?

ROB: It's very difficult for seminary students to think outside the hermeneutical method they've been taught on a particular verse and how to expositionally exegete it. I almost tend to work the opposite way. I have a text. I then ask myself, "Now where *in the world* is this text at work?" And the more random and the further out I can find this particular passage at work, the more beautiful and mysterious it will be.

DAVE: When I've heard you speak, you seem to drive home one line to your listeners. Is that repetition of a central theme intentional?

ROB: Yes. I'm actually not interested in leaving you with practical application. That is very low on my list of priorities because when I say, "This is what it means," then I feel like I'll always have to apply it for people.

Remember, rarely would the Rabbi answer a question. He'd respond with a question himself and then with another question. Often after a teaching, I'll say, "There are a couple of questions that this text forces me to ask." I'd rather leave you with an image so you see Scripture like a gem. You turn it and turn it and turn it, and the light refracts, and you see new things you didn't see before. I want to leave you with something that you may not get immediately. The practical application may kick in ten days later or a year later. I think great preaching *begins* the discussion, not *ends* it.

> **"I think great preaching *begins* the discussion, not *ends* it."**

The more you talk with Rob Bell, the more you'll find there truly is a method and meaning to his madness. Careful planning, preparation, and prayer get the message across. Rob always leaves people with some powerful image to accompany his powerful teaching. His audio clip on the CD forces you to think, and—as all his sermons do—he gives you an experience that's always outside the box.

Advice on Refining This Style

◆ *Be on the lookout for useful material.*

It's because of their passion for ministry that Unorthodox Artists are willing to learn from anyone, regardless of age or style. Rob learns from Letterman, Bono, and Beck. There isn't an air of superiority; he's open to all. Preaching patriarch Fred Craddock has said, "We ought to apprentice ourselves to all effective communicators—musicians, comedians, playwrights, news reporters, screenwriters, etc."[5]

Gifted communicators gather and assimilate quality material. They constantly sift through a variety of sources and styles and draw from each. To get started, listen to different types of music and observe commercials.

If you glean from outside your realm of knowledge, make certain you know what you're talking about. A friend of mine quoted the lyrics from an R.E.M. song in a sermon, but he incorrectly pronounced the group's name as "rim." Looking out for quality material is only half of the battle. The other half is doing your homework so that "everyone else's junk" (as Rob puts it) *enhances* the message.

◆ Invest in props.

If you really want to try this style, then don't skimp on your props. Props serve as visuals that listeners deposit into their memory banks. Make certain your audience can see them. If you have multiple services or classes, remember to set the props in place before each one.

Props can improve retention, but they lose their impact if you use one every week. Your audience will be thinking, "Oh boy, what did he pull out of his garage this week?" Ask yourself, "Is there a reason and purpose behind the prop?" If it's merely a distraction, don't use it.

◆ Think "substance," not "show."

The service's choreography can become a higher priority than the content. Unorthodoxy merely for the sake of being different grows old quickly; substance, though, has a lasting impact. If overdone, the arts or the element of shock will make your communication predictable rather than practical. So remember: The main thing is to keep the main thing the main thing.

> Unorthodoxy merely for the sake of being different grows old quickly.

Those who most effectively use this style have a method to their madness. They go the extra mile and carefully map out the "arc," or the reason for their unusual path.

Also, don't always feel the need to be unorthodox. Such pressure drains you and saps your creativity. This is one more reason that it's healthy to experiment with different styles of communication. If you periodically try different styles, you'll feed a variety of people in a variety of ways.

I consider Ed Young to be a creative genius. His unorthodox style is one of the keys to the growth of Fellowship Church. But he and Andy Stanley caution against overdoing it: "Excessive creative cramming results in a drowned audience. You've got to know when enough is enough and even when to cut back. Every so often—usually after a particularly multisensory weekend—we go back and do a simplistic service. We've found that a basic meat-and-potatoes message makes the more creative services stand out. Without balance you can lose perspective and fall into creative overload."[6]

◆ Make the Scriptures come alive.

Unorthodox Artists have a way of using creative methods to help their listeners realize the relevancy of the Word of God. They may use props to drive home a verse. A video clip from a popular movie may reinforce some biblical truth. Rob told about covering the stage with flowers so people could not only *hear* Solomon's words but they could also *see* the floral forms before them. You can do the same.

So get out of your box and take some risks—preferably well thought-out, prayed-out, and planned-out risks. Paul was right on target when he wrote, "So come on, let's leave the preschool fingerpainting exercises on Christ and get on with the grand work of art. Grow up in Christ" (Hebrews 6:1, *The Message*).

◆ Lead the audience to think and apply.

The Unorthodox Artist isn't concerned with an assembly line, cookie-cutter methodology. Instead, he or she is frenzied with scattering as many seeds as possible—and they may take awhile to germinate! "Great preaching *begins* the discussion, not *ends* it," Rob says. Preaching that leaves the dots unconnected prompts listeners to study and listen to the Holy Spirit on their own. Try an open-ended sermon in which the application intensifies after the message rather than during the message.

◆ Leave your audience with an image.

Ask yourself what picture you want to paint in the minds of your listeners. At my church, we sometimes refer to those as "Kodak moments." Once you know what mental picture you'd like your listeners to consider, plan your message to elicit that picture for the rest of the week.

ENDNOTES

1 Edwin B. Young and C. Andrew Stanley, *Can We Do That?: 24 Innovative Practices That Will Change the Way You Do Church* (West Monroe, LA: Howard Publishing Co. Inc., 2002), 151.

2 David A. Enyart, *Creative Anticipation: Narrative Sermon Designs for Telling the Story* (Philadelphia, PA: Xlibris Corporation, 2002), 31.

3 Rob Bell, "Life in Leviticus," Leadership magazine (Winter 2002, Vol. 24, No. 4), 45, from www.christianitytoday.com/le/2002/001/4.45.html.

4 Author's note: Rob also draws from an extensive list of commentaries and rabbinic resources on a regular basis.

5 Fred Craddock, comments (Indianapolis, IN: North American Christian Convention, July 10, 2003).

6 Young and Stanley, *Can We Do That?: 24 Innovative Practices That Will Change the Way You Do Church*, 157.

Epilogue

MY GOAL IN *REFINING YOUR STYLE* HAS BEEN TO ENCOURAGE YOU TO BE YOURSELF. Hopefully you've seen and heard yourself through the words of some excellent communicators. Perhaps a flame has been lit to improve your ability to preach and teach God's truth. You've learned some communication styles that are natural for you. No doubt you've been honest enough to acknowledge your weaknesses and strive to overcome them. If taken to heart and put into practice, these suggestions and your follow-through will help you to succeed in your calling.

For this book to have maximum impact, why not invite a respected peer to critique your communication? Honestly share your strengths and weaknesses, and see if he or she agrees with your assessment. Continue to listen to the CD to see how others communicate in their natural element.

There are four final applications that are necessary for me to share before this book finds a home on your shelf.

♦ *Your faithfulness and integrity supersede your style of communication.*

My desire for your preaching and teaching is that it becomes a natural outgrowth from your Christian life. Both Chuck Colson and Zig Ziglar tried to bring this out in their interviews. Michael Fabarez writes, "The personal life of the preacher is the foundation upon which his every sermon stands. [People's] defenses are bound to be up when we are perceived to be 'tinkering with one's soul.' We must never forget that preaching involves a kind of heart surgery that calls for the ultimate display of integrity on our part. They have every right to expect to find in us the lifestyle and relationship to God we are preaching about."[1] Who you are is more important than how you speak.

♦ *Recall* **what** *you do and* **why** *you do it.*

Take a journey back in time to the moment you sensed God laying on your heart a desire to communicate the good news. The summer after my sophomore year in Bible college, I did an internship with Southland Christian Church in Lexington, Kentucky. Part of our requirements for college credit was to keep a daily journal of practical lessons and observations. Although it meant some late night and early morning scribblings, those pages are valuable and meaningful to me. My favorite entry was written from a top bunk in a smelly cabin. It was a high school week of camp where I had just preached for the evening campfire service. After the message, one repentant camper even came forward, took a bag of marijuana out of his pocket, threw it in the fire, and said he wanted to change his life. This is what I wrote:

> I preached at campfire tonight—I didn't get to run through it beforehand. I had notes in my Bible and a flashlight, but I didn't end up using either. The Holy Spirit was in me, and I could feel him. I preached with more power than I ever had before. In the background were three illuminated crosses. Five people came forward and made decisions, and there is no doubt in my mind that I will preach the gospel until the day I die.

I wrote those words more than twenty-two years ago, but I could have written them today. I still feel compelled to preach the gospel until the day I die; in my opinion there is no higher calling.

◆ *Pray, anticipating God's presence.*

Bob Russell had lunch with David Foster, a Baptist preacher in Tennessee who has done extensive research on some of the largest churches in America. David said, "Bob, every church is so different. They each have their own worship style and their own goals. But there is one common thread. Do you know what that is?"

Bob said, "No, what is it?"

David said, "If you were to sit in the audience before the service starts and close your eyes, you wouldn't be able to tell which church you were in. There is this incredible sense of expectancy that is almost intoxicating."

When Bob shared that story with me, I couldn't get it out of my mind. I had to take it a step further. Regardless of the size of the church, that sensation should apply to the start of every worship service and specifically should describe the moment before any teaching time. As a communicator, I want that "incredible sense of expectancy" to be present every time you or I teach or preach. The listeners are on the edge of their seats because they anticipate the opening of God's Word and the feeding of their souls. The prayer in the minds of both speakers and listeners should be "What does God want to teach me today?"

◆ *Allow the Holy Spirit to work in and through you.*
A few months ago, I had one of those weeks in which my preparation time evaporated. Early in the week, I had conducted a high-profile funeral for a twenty-seven-year-old police officer who died in the line of duty. The next day, I'd been greeted with a fax from a newspaper showing a mug shot of a ministry friend who'd been arrested for possession of drugs. The aftermath of e-mails and phone calls left the well for writing a new sermon pretty dry. My preparation regimen had been thoroughly frazzled. Did I mention that it was the week after Easter, a record-breaking week with over twenty-eight thousand in attendance? Those who only recognize the sanctuary when it's covered in Easter lilies or poinsettias wouldn't be back until December, and that reality served as another downer to decelerate my sermon preparation.

Our regular Thursday afternoon staff meeting to review my sermon manuscript was so discouraging that we scheduled another meeting for the next morning. My mentor read my manuscript, looked across the table, and said in a serious voice, "You've got a lot of work to do." Ouch.

The group called *another* meeting for the next day. This was a first in my fifteen years of preaching at Southeast. While the extra help was appreciated, the mere fact that we met again on Friday didn't bolster my self-confidence.

Since my text was the Acts 1 passage on the ascension of Christ, I decided to focus on the fact that unless Jesus had left us, he wouldn't have sent the Holy Spirit. Rather than deity being limited to one location, the Spirit of God could dwell in the life of *every* person who puts his or her trust in Jesus Christ. I didn't feel great about the sermon; I felt good that although it had come slowly, I'd stuck with it.

As I drove home after preaching, my cell phone rang. It was my wife, who was about five miles ahead of me on the same road. She said, "Great sermon. There's somebody here who has some good news that he'd like to talk with you about today." The next voice I heard was that of my eight-year-old son, Samuel. He said, "Dad, I want to give my life to Jesus."

Words cannot describe the feelings behind the lump in my throat when I heard those words. After I congratulated him and told him how proud I was of him, my wife got back on the phone.

Beth said, "When he looked up at me during the invitation, he had tears in his eyes, and he said, 'I'm ready to become a Christian and be baptized.'"

Beth had asked him, "Samuel, do you want that Spirit that Dad talked about living inside of you?" He'd nodded and said "yes." Beth said that his tears dripped down onto the concrete sanctuary floor.

While I drove five miles behind them on the same interstate, somehow his tears became my tears. It was tough to see the road. Not only was my son embarking on the most important decision of his life, but God was teaching a veteran preacher a fresh lesson: *The Holy Spirit will always convey a personal message to those who are open to receiving it.*

As I had labored and struggled for hours over that message, I'd fallen into a trap. I thought I was crafting the message for a crowd of eighteen thousand people. I was mistaken. God intended for it to touch the heart of my one and only son, who on that day realized he was a sinner in need of a Savior. You never know who will respond or how the Spirit will communicate through your style, so be faithful and diligent in your preparation.

As you've read this book, you've been reminded of the gift of communication God has given you. Your natural style is merely the vehicle God will use to allow the Holy Spirit to speak through you.

Years ago when I entered the ministry, an older man said to me, "Follow the grain in your own wood." That was good advice then and good advice now. Galli and Larson sum it up well: "*You are the unique thing you bring to the pulpit.* Certainly you aim to interpret the text faithfully, and you want to preach Christ and not yourself. But it is *you* who preaches Christ. And you will preach Christ a little differently than any other preacher. Not to do so is to deny your God-given uniqueness."[2]

So open, illustrate, apply, and preach the Word. Refine your style where needed, but remember to be yourself. After all, no one can do that any better than you. Before you stand to communicate the gospel, it's my prayer that you will remember Søren Kierkegaard's wonderful prayer: "Now, with God's help, I shall become myself."[3]

ENDNOTES

1 Michael Fabarez, *Preaching That Changes Lives* (Nashville, TN: Thomas Nelson Inc., 2002), 25-26. Used by permission of Thomas Nelson, Inc.

2 Taken from PREACHING THAT CONNECTS by CRAIG BRIAN LARSON; MARK GALLI. Copyright © 1994 by Mark Galli and Craig Brian Larson. Used by permission of The Zondervan Corporation.

3 John Ortberg, *The Life You've Always Wanted: Spiritual Disciplines for Ordinary People* (Grand Rapids, MI: Zondervan), 11. Quoting Søren Kierkegaard in *The Prayers of Kierkegaard*, Perry LeFevre, ed. (Chicago: University of Chicago Press, 1956), 147.

About the CD

THE BONUS CD ACCOMPANYING THIS BOOK COMPRISES EXCERPTS from messages delivered by many of the speakers I interviewed. The messages were delivered in a variety of settings and were recorded with several kinds of recording equipment, which accounts for the acoustical variations you will detect.

1. Erwin McManus, excerpt from a message delivered during the Youth Specialties Conference on February 15-16, 2002, in San Diego, California.

2. Charles Colson, excerpt from a message delivered during the main session of the Praise Gathering on October 10, 2002, in Indianapolis, Indiana.

3. Timothy J. Keller, excerpt from "Enduring Grace," a message delivered on March 10, 2002, at Redeemer Presbyterian Church in New York, New York.

4. Max Lucado, excerpt from "Come Thirsty—You Can't Give What You Don't Receive," a message delivered on August 3, 2003, at Oak Hills Church in San Antonio, Texas (Upwords Tape Ministry).

5. Kirbyjon Caldwell, excerpt from "Sailing the Seas of Life," a message delivered on September 21, 2003, at Windsor Village United Methodist Church in Houston, Texas.

6. Gene Appel, excerpt from "More Like Jesus," a message delivered on February 25, 2003, at the Ozark Christian College Preaching/Teaching Convention in Joplin, Missouri.

7. Rob Bell, excerpt from "The Cross, Part 3: Dying to Live," a message delivered on October 12, 2003, at Mars Hill Bible Church in Grandville, Michigan.

8. Liz Curtis Higgs, excerpt from "A Heart Lesson from Leah," a message delivered on May 10, 2003, in Detroit, Michigan.

9. Bob Russell, excerpt from "Ruth and Naomi—Unlikely Friends," a message delivered on November 2, 2003, at Southeast Christian Church in Louisville, Kentucky.

10. Zig Ziglar, excerpt from "Spiritual Journey," a message delivered in 1995. Used by permission of Ziglar Training Systems, 2009 Chenault Drive, Suite 100, Carrollton, TX 75006. All rights reserved.

11. Ken Davis, excerpt from a presentation on September 18, 2003, in Hays, Kansas.

12. Dave Stone, excerpt from "Pursue Reconciliation," a message delivered on August 24, 2003, at Southeast Christian Church, Louisville, Kentucky.

Resource Page for
Our Featured Communicators

Gene Appel: www.willowcreek.org

Rob Bell: www.marshillbiblechurch.org and www.nooma.com

Kirbyjon Caldwell: www.kingdombuilder.com

Charles Colson: www.pfm.org

Ken Davis: www.kendavis.com

Liz Curtis Higgs: www.lizcurtishiggs.com

Franklin Graham: www.samaritanspurse.org

Tim Keller: www.redeemer.com

Max Lucado: www.maxlucado.com

Erwin McManus: www.mosaic.org

Bob Russell: www.southeastchristian.org and
www.livingword.org

Dave Stone: www.southeastchristian.org and
www.preachingplus.com and www.livingword.org

Zig Ziglar: www.zigziglar.com

EVALUATION FOR

Refining Your Style

Please help Group Publishing, Inc., continue to provide innovative and useful resources for ministry. Please take a moment to fill out this evaluation and mail or fax it to us. Thanks!

Group Publishing, Inc.
Attention: Product Development
P.O. Box 481
Loveland, CO 80539
Fax: (970) 292-4370

● ● ●

1. As a whole, this book has been (circle one)

not very helpful   *very helpful*

  1   2   3   4   5   6   7   8   9   10

2. The best things about this book:

3. Ways this book could be improved:

4. Things I will change because of this book:

5. Other books I'd like to see Group publish in the future:

6. Would you be interested in field-testing future Group products and giving us your feedback? If so, please fill in the information below:

Name _____

Church Name _____

Denomination _____ Church Size _____

Church Address _____

City _____ State _____ ZIP _____

Church Phone _____

E-mail _____